D1795312

Essential Business Law

Defective Goods

General Editor of the Series:
Maurice Kay

Other Titles in the Series:
Agency in Commerce
Arbitration
Company Finance, Takeovers and Mergers
Company Insolvency
Company Structure
Consumer Credit
Family Businesses and Partnerships
Insurance
International Trade
Law and the Legal System
Leases of Business Premises

AUSTRALIA
The Law Book Company Ltd.
Sydney: Melbourne: Brisbane

CANADA AND U.S.A.
The Carswell Company Ltd.
Agincourt, Ontario

INDIA
N. M. Tripathi Private Ltd.
Bombay
and
Eastern Law House (Private) Ltd.
Calcutta
M.P.P. House
Bangalore

ISRAEL
Steimatzky's Agency Ltd.
Jerusalem: Tel Aviv: Haifa

MALAYSIA: SINGAPORE: BRUNEI
Malayan Law Journal (Pte.) Ltd.
Singapore

NEW ZEALAND
Sweet & Maxwell (N.Z.) Ltd.
Auckland

PAKISTAN
Pakistan Law House
Karachi

Essential Business Law

Defective Goods

Michael Whincup

LONDON
SWEET & MAXWELL
1979

Published in 1979 by
Sweet & Maxwell Limited of
11 New Fetter Lane, London
Computerset by
MFK Graphic Systems (Typesetting) Ltd., Saffron Walden
Printed in Great Britain by
Hazell Watson & Viney Ltd., Aylesbury

ISBN 0 421 24680 4

SERIES INTRODUCTION

In the last 15 years Businessmen and Managers have had to come to terms with a vast increase in the volume and complexity of laws affecting their activities. As a response to this there is a growing demand for courses, conferences and other literature, which explain these laws to those most directly affected by them. Many lawyers have helped to satisfy this demand but, in so doing, they have often presented the material as "lawyers' law."

Essential Business Law is a series of small books specifically designed to present some of the most important areas of business law to businessmen. The Series is not intended to be comprehensive, nor will it make instant lawyers. However, it is hoped that by adding to its readers' understanding of the legal fabric of business, it will help to make them better businessmen.

Defective Goods is a general guide to our rights and duties as shoppers, retailers or manufacturers. With illustrations from decided cases, it explains the law, not only on quality, fitness and safety of goods, but also as it affects the supply of services. Other important and interesting features include a discussion of how and when a contract is made, the new law on unfair contract terms, rules against deceptive advertising and "hard sell" techniques, and a summary of legal aid entitlement.

In Memory of Hans Bergqvist

CONTENTS

AUTHOR'S NOTE

THE Sale of Goods Act 1893 is repealed and re-enacted, with later amendments, by the Sale of Goods Bill 1979. This Bill leaves unaltered the section numbers of the old Act, but will make it unnecessary to refer separately to the Misrepresentation Act or Supply of Goods (Implied Terms) Act.

CHAPTER ONE
MAKING AND BREAKING CONTRACTS

Introduction

A consumer's rights under English law depend in the first place on whether he has suffered a civil or criminal wrong. Broadly the purpose of civil law is to compensate the victim and that of the criminal law to punish the wrongdoer. Broadly also we can say in the context of consumer law that problems of defective goods are civil matters while the rules on advertising and certain sales techniques are laid down primarily by the criminal law. In the first five chapters we shall be concerned with civil rights—rights which the consumer must exert for himself—and in Chapter Six with the ways advertising and other sales pressures are controlled by local authorities and the Office of Fair Trading. Civil rights in turn differ considerably according to whether the consumer's grievance concerns a breach of contract, *e.g.* where an injured buyer sues the seller (Chapters Two and Three), or some non-contractual wrong, as where it is the buyer's child who is injured by the goods; Chapter Four.

The first thing we have to establish therefore is what a contract is, how and when it is made, and what the remedies are for breaking it. What follows is not an "Outline of the Law of Contract," but is intended only to answer these basic questions—pointing out in passing a few likely pitfalls and common areas of misunderstanding.

What is an Enforceable Contract?

A contract is not the easiest thing in the world to define. There is no statutory or other decisive statement of what it involves. One could say indeed that contract law is whatever you care to make it. This may seem a rather strange proposition, but it is essentially true. If you and I make a contract and one of us breaks it, for whatever reason, the innocent party goes to court (if he can afford

1

to go that far, a question considered in Chapter Seven) so that the judge may order the other party: "Carry out your contract—or else . . . !" In other words, *the law is the contract*. What actually goes into the contract is another matter, depending largely on each side's bargaining power. A monopoly or other economically strong seller can impose terms on a weaker party which might be unacceptable in a more competitive situation. The law intervenes here and there, as we shall see, to protect the weak but it is certainly neither concerned nor able to ensure that everyone gets what he personally might regard as a fair deal. So far as prices are concerned, for example, shopkeepers are free to charge whatever they please—subject to the courts' power to reopen "extortion-ate" credit transactions (section 139, Consumer Credit Act, 1974), and to what is said below about situations where a "reasonable" price has to be fixed. Complaints about profiteer-ing may, however, be made to the Office of Fair Trading, which can investigate abuses of market power. And we might also note in passing that the prices of bread, butter, milk and paraffin are controlled by statute.

Despite the difficulties of definition, however, we can say with reasonable confidence that when a judge is asked to enforce an agreement he will have in mind certain basic "ingredients" or prerequisites of enforceability. In English law at least there seem to be four main factors, which interlock and overlap each other. The first is what the parties intended; the second, whether they have expressed their intentions with sufficient clarity; third, whether there was an offer and acceptance, and finally whether "consideration" was given. We shall see as we go along that writing is usually only important as evidence of these factors and not itself a vital contractual requirement.

(i) *Intention*

It goes almost without saying that in deciding contract cases our judges wish to give effect to the parties' intentions. But there are many practical difficulties in the way of simply asking each party "What was the purpose of this contract?" and then holding liable whichever one prevented its fulfilment. If someone with little bargaining power, who has to accept the terms imposed upon him or do without, were asked whether he "intended" to make a bad bargain he would no doubt say that he did not, but how much importance should we attach to that? With the best will in the world judges cannot remedy every inequality or rewrite every agreement. Nor, to put it another way round, would it be either fair or feasible to compel large organisations which may make thousands of contracts a day—such as British Rail—to re-negotiate their terms with each and every passenger instead of being able to rely on standard form conditions.

Parliament has, however, intervened to lay down minimum standards governing many different types of contract. Familiar examples include the Rent Acts, Employment Protection Act, Factories Act and so on. In consumer protection probably the most vital measures are the Sale of Goods Act, 1893, as amended by the Supply of Goods (Implied Terms) Act, 1973, The Consumer Credit Act, 1974, and the Unfair Contract Terms Act, 1977, the relevant parts of which are all discussed in the following chapters. The Sale of Goods Act is particularly important because as we shall see it provides implied terms of fitness in all commercial sales. It also says what the appropriate remedies are for breach of these requirements, which we shall discuss at the end of this chapter.

Terms may be implied for other reasons too, such as the parties' failure to say what should happen in certain circumstances which have now occurred. If the problem is not one regulated by Act of Parliament but has indeed arisen because of some oversight or error by the parties, it is for the judge himself to decide what if any term he should add to the contract to resolve the difficulty. But he can only add terms if it is actually *necessary* to do so to save an otherwise meaningful and binding agreement from being nullified; *Liverpool City Council* v. *Irwin*, 1976. Examples are given in Chapter Three. Of course, if the judge does decide to add a term to a contract on that basis it may not be one which the parties would have agreed to had they thought about it in the first place. To that extent again therefore the intentions of the parties may be overridden—though only, one might say, in order to make sense of their agreement.

Another aspect of this question—and probably one of the commonest reasons for going to law—is that what the parties say or write may be differently interpreted, and each now interprets the agreement to suit himself. Such problems are almost impossible to avoid. Even when technical specifications are used differences of opinion still arise. Again there is always the possibility that contracting parties may say one thing but mean another. How far can the judge go to find their real wishes? Inevitably the case must be decided on what they have openly said or written rather than on what they privately hoped or believed, otherwise contracts would be worthless. This approach may, nonetheless, lead to conclusions quite contrary to their actual intentions; *Rose* v. *Pim*, 1953.

Again, while the purpose and terms may be perfectly clear the judge may sometimes say the parties did not intend the agreement to be legally binding and will refuse to enforce it accordingly. He may refuse either because the parties expressly said their bargain was "binding in honour only" or a "gentlemen's agreement"—or other such optimistic phraseology—or because of surrounding circumstances. Legal enforcement of domestic or social agreements, for example, is almost a contradiction in terms, unless perhaps large sums of money are involved and/or family or neighbourly relations are already strained and formal; *Simpkins* v. *Pays*, 1955. And even what look like business deals may be invalidated because of their informality. So the absence of written evidence in circumstances where writing would normally be expected might occasionally suggest that the parties did not regard their agreement as finalised or binding; *Licences Insurance Corp.* v. *Lawson*, 1896.

An interesting and important question in sales law is whether advertisements are intended to be binding, or should be so in any event. Usually they cannot be binding because they are just statements of opinion; goods are said to be "bigger" or "better" or "whiter" or "faster" without any standards by which such opinions or "puff" could be tested. But conversely if advertisements state *facts* which can be tested, there is no reason why they should not be enforced as contractual promises. So in *Carlill* v. *Carbolic Smoke Ball Co.*, 1893, manufacturers were bound by an express promise in their advertisement to pay £100 to anyone who used their concoction but nevertheless caught 'flu. Strangely enough, however, a statement may be factual in one context, but not in another. A dealer's glowing description of a new car, for instance, might be mere puff because he clearly could not say whether this model was more reliable or effective than any other, but if he said the same thing about a used car he could be liable

4

for breach of contract because he has examined that car himself and should know about its quality or condition; *Andrews* v. *Hopkinson*, 1957. Sales literature, price lists and the like often disclaim contractual effect, not necessarily because what they say is untrue but because the manufacturer reserves the right to change his materials or specifications over a period of time. Alternatively, the conditions of sale themselves may make it clear that the parties are contracting only on the basis of what is agreed there and then, and that nothing said previously in advertisements or the like is of any significance at all. This may seem like sharp practice, since it is probably in reliance on the advertisement that the customer buys the goods, but the law permits exclusion of liability for pre-contractual statements if it is reasonable to do so in the circumstances. We shall see what that involves when we look at the Unfair Contract Terms Act in Chapter Five.

Another possibility is that advertisements or other sales talk may be classed as "representations"—a kind of half-way house between puffs which have no legal effect and the binding terms of the contract itself. A representation is a statement of fact which encourages or induces a person to make a contract but which does not necessarily form part of that contract. It would probably be a representation to say, for example, that a car has had only one previous owner or has done such-and-such a mileage. If the statement is subsequently proved wrong, the buyer's remedy depends on whether the misrepresentation was made fraudulently, negligently, or innocently. He is entitled to repudiate the contract and/or claim damages for fraudulent misrepresentation. The Misrepresentation Act, 1967, allows a claim for damages for negligent or innocent misrepresentation, and/or the buyer might possibly be able to rescind the contract—*i.e.* give back the goods and recover his money. But if the buyer has used the goods to any extent or otherwise seems to have accepted them, that cannot be done; *Long* v. *Lloyd*, 1958.

The criminal law and the Office of Fair Trading both have very important parts to play in controlling advertising. These are described in Chapter Six.

(ii) *Certainty*
The second main ingredient of enforceability is that the wording of the contract is clear enough to enable the judge to give effect to

5

the parties' wishes—a requirement overlapping that of intention, above. Phrases such as "at a price to be agreed" or "on the usual h.p. terms" invite disaster—unless the contract has actually been carried out by one or both parties. If goods have been delivered as requested they have to be paid for, and if no price has yet been agreed the judge must decide what is a "reasonable" price on all the available evidence; *Foley* v. *Classique Coaches*, 1934. An "estimate" may well be enforceable, unless there is some agreement to the contrary; *Croshaw* v. *Pritchard*, 1889. Promises to "use one's best endeavours" and the like are probably too vague to be enforceable. Agreements expressed in "letters of intent" or as "subject to contract" are similarly inconclusive, unless perhaps acted on by one party to the knowledge and benefit of the other—*Turiff* v. *Regalia Mills*, 1971—or when the phrase "subject to contract" is used to mean that the parties intend to put in writing commitments already agreed by word of mouth. If so the mere change in form does not affect the validity of the existing agreement. While written evidence is always preferable, it is only *essential* in land, hire purchase and a few other exceptional transactions. One can never be quite sure, however, what the effect of an omission or an obscure or meaningless term will be. A contract which is clear and self-sufficient in all other respects will not be invalidated just because one sentence is doubtful, and details are not always necessary if the basic obligation is clear; *Sykes* v. *Fine Fare*, 1966. Each case must depend on its own merits.

(iii) *Offer and Acceptance*
On the face of it an agreement is a "meeting of minds" between the parties—a "consensus"—though as we have seen that consensus may be more apparent than real. The basic elements of agreement are an offer by one party to buy or sell goods or services on certain terms and an acceptance of those terms by the other. But there is, of course, no need to say formally "This is an offer" or "I accept your offer" and indeed the use of those words may sometimes be quite misleading; *Bigg* v. *Boyd Gibbins*, 1971. Agreement may in appropriate circumstances be inferred simply from a person's conduct, *e.g.* when he gets on a bus.

The law does not regard a display of goods in a shop window or a statement of their price as an offer. So a customer who queues all night for a sales bargain still cannot demand the goods, because legally the display is only an invitation to him to come in and make an offer for the goods, which the shopkeeper can then accept or reject as he thinks fit—even in a self-service store. (But if the shopkeeper rejects the offer by putting the price up he commits an offence under the Trade Descriptions Act; Chapter Six.) When a customer buys petrol at a self-service garage, however, it seems that the petrol price display is an offer which the customer accepts by filling his tank. The usual rule is reversed here because once the petrol is in the tank it cannot be recovered, and so there can be no more bargaining by the garage. If goods are delivered or work done without the other side's express or implied consent, *e.g.* when a new engine is fitted in the course of what is supposed to be an ordinary car service, no offer has been made and so the customer is not obliged to accept. See also the Unsolicited Goods and Services Act; Chapter Six.

Offers lapse unless accepted reasonably quickly; *Ramsgate Hotel* v. *Montefiore*, 1866. An offer can be withdrawn at any time before acceptance, even if the person to whom it is made suffers loss by relying on a promise to keep it open; *Routledge* v. *Grant*, 1828. Acceptance by post is complete once the letter is posted (unlike offers and revocations of offers), unless perhaps the letter is wrongly addressed or the offer says the letter of acceptance must actually be received. An offer can only be validly accepted *as it stands*. If the buyer and seller are agreed on all the terms and then the buyer says: "I'll take the goods if you can deliver them within a week," that may well be a new term, in effect a counter-offer, which effectively nullifies the original offer. If the seller rejects the counter-offer, in legal theory at any rate the whole agreement must then be renegotiated; *Northland Airlines* v. *Ferranti*, 1970. Or of course the buyer might say "I'll take the goods. Can you deliver them within a week?" If that is merely a request for information or for a service the buyer would prefer but does not insist upon, the original contract is not affected; *Stevenson* v. *Mclean*, 1880. Another version of the problem arises when the buyer writes off for goods on such-and-such terms and the seller replies with standard form conditions of sale which contradict the buyer's offer. If the buyer makes no objection and accepts the goods he is presumed to have accepted the seller's counter-offer; *B.R.S.* v. *Crutchley*, 1968. But once the contract is complete neither side can vary it without further agreement; *Evans* v. *Merzario*, 1976.

It is clearly safer and more sensible to try to reach agreement formally, particularly in complex or expensive transactions, with each side knowing and recording the terms. But more often than not in practice it is simply one man's word against another as to what has been said or done, and the judge must decide whom he believes.

(iv) Valuable Consideration

So far what we have called the ingredients of an enforceable contract have been largely matters of common sense—that the parties mean what they say, express themselves clearly, and are agreed upon their bargain. The fourth ingredient is more strictly a requirement of law and less obviously one of common sense. It is a basic rule of English law (albeit with certain exceptions) that a contractual relationship is essentially one imposing obligations on both parties—that a contract requires a *bargain*, and not just a promise. In effect the law says that A's promise to do something for B is not binding upon him unless B does something in return for that promise. What B does or gives in return is called consideration for A's promise, and only by giving it can B enforce that promise. Putting it shortly, B must "buy" A's promise before he can enforce it. The consideration he gives may take many different forms. Usually it is a promise in return for a promise—*e.g.* a promise to work in return for a promise to pay—but it can equally well involve a payment or an act, or a detriment or forebearance of any kind, as long as what is done or given up is of some economic value—though not necessarily equivalent to the value of the promise or goods or services it buys. With reservations noted in Chapter Five, English law is not interested in the *fairness* of the bargain, only in seeing that there is a bargain *of some sort*. It is a curious fact then that while Englishmen have gone round the world proclaiming "An Englishman's word is his bond" the law has been quietly saying that that simply isn't so at all!

This requirement of mutuality or reciprocity produces many complications and occasional injustice. In particular, and subject to what is said below on "estoppel," it is not enough simply to rely on a man's promise, as we saw earlier in *Routledge* v. *Grant*. Acting "in reliance on" and acting "in return for" another's promise are legally speaking two entirely different propositions, and only the second is consideration. Again, if buyer and seller have struck a bargain and the seller then gives some further assurance about the quality of the goods which turns out to be untrue the buyer cannot sue him for breach of that promise because his own consideration—the payment or promise of payment—was given *before* and without reference to the final assurance; *Roscorla* v. *Thomas*, 1842. But that does not, of course, affect the validity of agreement on the price of goods which is not reached until after they have been delivered, because in all probability the promise to pay was implied from the start; *Re Cassey's Patents*, 1892. One particular aspect of the problem concerns the enforcement of manufacturers' guarantees, a question pursued in Chapter Four.

Estoppel

It might seem that without consideration no rights at all can arise under a contract, but every rule has exceptions. The principle of "estoppel" is that if a person makes a promise intending someone to act on it, who does act upon it as intended, the promisor is prevented—estopped—from going back on his promise *even though the promisee gave no consideration for it*; *Central London Property Trust* v. *High Trees House*, 1947. A creditor who allowed a debtor more time to pay therefore could not sue the debtor for not paying by the date originally agreed—so long as the creditor's agreement was voluntary; *D. & C. Builders* v. *Rees*, 1966. But the estoppel rule does not go so far as to make consideration unnecessary; it simply stops the promisor from suing the promisee as if he had never made his promise. If it were the promisee who wanted to sue the promisor he would still have to show he had given consideration, and as we said earlier acting in reliance on a promise, as distinct from doing something in return for it, is not consideration; *Combe* v. *Combe*, 1951. There may possibly be exceptions, however, even to this exception. A person might be able to sue on a promise for which he has not given consideration, if that is the only way he can maintain the situation as the other person promised it would be, or protect the rights the other promised but now seeks to take away; *Crabb* v. *Arun R.D.C.*, 1975.

Summary

These at all events are the four basic requirements of contract law—intention to be bound, certainty, offer and acceptance and valuable consideration. At that point in time when they can all be found together an enforceable contract comes into being. With exceptions we have noted, and subject to the "cooling-off" provisions mentioned in Chapter Six, it does not matter that the agreement is not in writing, nor that payment may be postponed, nor that the contract as a whole is not to be carried out until some distant future date. If a buyer tells a seller that he will pay £X for the goods and will be back to collect them the following day, when on closer inspection he changes his mind, he is thereupon in breach of contract. The contract was made when he said he would take them, and broken when he rejected them. As to the question of compensating the seller for his loss, see Remedies, below.

Before we leave these requirements altogether, however, there is just one other point we ought to make, which will show once again that no rule is sacred or self-sufficient. Even where there is no concluded agreement at all some remedy might still be given for what might be called "disappointed expectation." If I know you are going to considerable trouble and expense on my behalf in the reasonable belief or expectation that a contract has been or will be made between us, and I take the benefit of your work but do not make that contract, the cases show that I must pay you for the work you have done; *Lacey* v. *Davis*, 1957.

The Terms of the Contract: Conditions and Warranties
In later chapters we shall look at contracts for the sale and hire purchase of goods and the provision of services and discuss there the kinds of obligations which may be expressly agreed by the parties or imposed by law. At this introductory stage, however, we should note how the law describes or classifies these obligations. For many years the practice has been to divide them into "conditions" and "warranties"—in effect the distinction between fundamental terms and those of less significance. On breach of condition the innocent party may repudiate the contract and/or claim damages, whereas on a breach of warranty the innocent party, having got more or less what he asked for, must go on with his side of the agreement but can reduce his payment or claim damages for any deficiencies. It may not be easy to say in advance whether any particular term is a condition or warranty, and over the past few years the courts have preferred to say that

terms which are not so classified are "intermediate" or "innominate" stipulations. The appropriate remedy can then be decided in the light of the consequences of breach of that term: *Hong Kong Fir Shipping Co.* v. *Kawasaki*, 1962. This is a more rational approach, but unfortunately it conflicts with both the Sale of Goods Act and Consumer Credit Act which classify certain implied terms as either conditions or warranties, regardless of the actual effects of breach. The difficulties caused thereby will be seen in the next chapter. We might note also that if the words "condition" or "warranty" are used in contracts the judges will not interpret them in their strict legal sense unless satisfied that the parties intended to use them in that sense and were aware of the consequences; *Wickman* v. *Schuler*, 1974. But on the other hand again if there is no doubt that the parties do mean what they say—if, for example, payment expressly depends on complete and exact performance of the contract—then a relatively minor fault which would otherwise only give rise to a claim for damages might have to be treated as a breach of condition. Cases of this kind are discussed in Chapter Three, while in Chapter Five we shall see how far the supplier can avoid liability for breach of condition or warranty by the terms of the contract.

Remedies for Breach of Contract: Damages and Repudiation
The principal remedies for breach of contract are as above those of repudiation and/or damages, depending on either the seriousness of the breach or the prior classification of the term in question by Act of Parliament or by the parties themselves. We should observe first therefore that neither of the remedies which most dissatisfied buyers want—repair or replacement of defective goods—is recognised as such by English law, though often endorsed by Continental systems. But if the buyer is entitled to repudiate or claim damages he can of course ask for repair or replacement in lieu and would appear bound by the terms of any such settlement if it is satisfactorily carried out by the seller. Very occasionally a consumer may feel he must demonstrate publicly against alleged bad service. If so he should guard against liability for public nuisance, defamation, etc.; *Crest* v. *Ascott*, 1975.

So far as strict legal rights are concerned, however, one other possible remedy should be noted—that of an order for specific performance. The purpose of this order is to compel the party in breach to carry out the contract as he promised. Such orders are rare. Damages are usually sufficient to make up for any loss the innocent party may have suffered, and in any case the courts are not equipped to supervise people to see they keep their promises. But where the subject matter of the contract is unique or exceptional in some way and damages inadequate, *e.g.* a plot of land, specific performance may be ordered.

It follows that awards of damages are much the most common remedy, and we shall now outline some of the basic rules on the subject. Finally, we shall say a little more about the other major—but of the nature of things less common—remedy of repudiation.

The purpose of an award of damages is that "where a party sustains a loss by reason of a breach of contract he is, so far as money can do it, to be placed in the same situation . . . as if the contract had been performed"; *Robinson* v. *Harman*, 1848. But a successful plaintiff may still be left out of pocket for several reasons—perhaps because of the impossibility of calculating his losses exactly, or the rules on remoteness of damage, mitigation and the like we are about to discuss, or simply because of costs—the rules on which, although largely beyond the scope of this book, usually ensure that the winner must pay at least part of his own legal fees; Chapter Seven.

Remoteness

Once the court is satisfied a contract has been made and one or more of its terms broken, and that the breach has caused loss to the plaintiff, its most difficult task is to decide *which consequences* of the breach should be compensated. Only after this question of "remoteness" has been resolved can the court calculate the "quantum" or amount. A distinction must be drawn between direct consequences and those so indirect or unpredictable that it would be unjust to burden the defendant with them. The direct consequences are those normally arising from such a breach, or those additional or abnormal losses which these particular parties had or should have had in mind: *Hadley* v. *Baxendale*, 1854; *Victoria Laundry* v. *Newman*, 1949: *Koufos* v. *Czarnikow*, 1969. As between buyer and seller of goods these common law rules are enlarged upon by sections 49–54 of the Sale of Goods Act. A buyer who wrongfully refuses to pay for goods once they are his is liable for the price. If he wrongfully refuses to accept them the seller should sell elsewhere and claim the difference, if any; *Lazenby* v. *Wright*, 1976. If in either case the buyer put down a deposit the seller may be content to keep that sum, which he is entitled to do if the deposit is a promise of completion—subject to his duty to reduce his loss, below. Conversely if the seller fails to deliver the goods the buyer should obtain some elsewhere and the seller is liable for the difference in price. Usually, therefore, the current market price is the yardstick by which damages are assessed. But the market price may not be a realistic guide if supply exceeds demand; *Thompson* v. *Robinson*, 1955; *Charter* v. *Sullivan*, 1957.

Damages can be claimed for other "direct and natural" consequential expenses such as repairs, loss of use, storage, medical expenses, the innocent buyer's costs in defending himself against claims brought by sub-purchasers, and so on; *H.L. Motor Works* v. *Alwahbi*, 1977. If the direct result of the defect is physical injury, compensation is likewise due. So in *Godley* v. *Perry*, 1960, a child who bought a catapult which broke when he used it and blinded him in one eye was awarded £2,500 against the shopkeeper. It is sufficient that *some* damage or injury is the likely consequence of the defect, and not necessary to prove that what actually happened was foreseen; *Parsons* v. *Uttley Ingham*, 1978. Compensation may also be ordered for more nebulous matters such as inconvenience, discomfort, disappointment or injured feelings; *Heywood* v. *Wellers*, 1976—solicitor liable for distress and inconvenience caused to client by his incompetence. Other important cases in this connection are *Jarvis* v. *Swan's Tours*, 1973, and *Jackson* v. *Horizon Holidays*, 1975, referred to in Chapter Three on contracts for service. *Jackson* establishes also that where one person makes a contract for the benefit of another, *e.g.* a husband booking a holiday for himself and his family, he can sue on the other's behalf for loss or injury suffered. But if the goods or services are not so clearly obtained for someone else's benefit the rule is that one can only claim for one's own losses; *Lockett* v. *Charles*, 1935: *Priest* v. *Last*, 1903—husband whose wife was scalded by a hot water bottle he had bought could not claim against the seller for her injuries but only for the expenses he had incurred in looking after her.

Mitigation

Another basic rule but one we need not pursue in detail is that the law expects the victim of a breach of contract to do his best to reduce or "mitigate" his own losses. If a seller fails to deliver goods his buyer who wishes to use them for profit must try immediately to obtain similar goods elsewhere, and if a buyer refuses to accept delivery the seller must try to find another buyer. Inaction will reduce any damages which might otherwise be awarded. But if reasonable attempts to mitigate loss only make matters worse the further expense is recoverable.

Anticipatory Breach

An anticipatory breach occurs where one party to the contract makes clear before the due day that he is not going to carry out his promise. The innocent party then has a choice. He may either accept the repudiation, refuse to carry out his own obligations and claim damages for the loss he has suffered *at the date of repudiation*, subject to his duty to mitigate his loss, or treat the contract as still in being, and claim (probably more substantial) damages for the loss he sustains *at the time it should have been carried out*. The difficulty arising from this choice is that the second course of action flatly contradicts the duty to mitigate, as illustrated in *White and Carter* v. *McGregor*, 1962. According to this case a buyer who has second thoughts and cancels his order immediately after making it may still be liable to the seller for the seller's total loss of profit on the transaction—a surprising and indeed alarming conclusion!

Repudiation

We have said that if either side breaks a condition of the contract, as defined above, the innocent party can repudiate the agreement. If he is the buyer, for example, he can refuse to pay for the defective goods and leave the seller to recover them. But section 11 of the Sale of Goods Act which gives him this right also says that where the contract of sale is not severable (*i.e.* cannot be divided into separate and independent parts) and the buyer has accepted the goods or part of them, he loses his right to reject and can only claim damages, unless the contract provides otherwise. It is a proposition of common sense as well as law that a buyer who accepts goods cannot then reject them—but what is "acceptance"? By section 35 the buyer accepts goods by saying so, or, having had the opportunity to examine them, by actions implying acceptance, *e.g.* resale, or "when after the lapse of a reasonable time he retains the goods without intimating to the seller that he has rejected them." In practice this is the problem area. How long is a "reasonable time"? A car buyer, for example, could not expect to give the vehicle back as soon as the first fault appeared. What matters is the cumulative effect of the faults, which might take months to appear. It would be wrong to penalise the buyer in such circumstances. In one of the cases considered in the next chapter, *Farnworth Finance* v. *Attryde*, 1970, four months' use and several thousand miles' driving were held not to constitute acceptance, because during this time many attempts were made, but failed, to cure a series of lethal defects. Similarly in *Spencer* v. *Rye*, 1972, three months' possession and intermittent use was no bar, because the car still would not go. In *Lightburn* v. *Belmont*, 1969 (Can.), the judge allowed rescission even though the buyer had driven the car 8,000 miles in eight months. His reasons were that "Mr. Lightburn was endeavouring to give the car a reasonable chance to perform and I do not agree that delay in finally repudiating his contract can be attributed to that period of time or the mileage that was covered. He was not acting as a capricious buyer who has repented the purchase and sought to get out of his contract at an early time on a frivolous basis." These considerations are surely the right ones—not only in the sense that they give relief where it is needed but also in obliging buyers generally to try to "make a go" of their contracts. Decisions going the other way include *Charterhouse Credit* v. *Tolly*, 1963, and *Lee* v. *York Coach*, 1977. In both cases serious defects in the vehicles were discovered shortly after delivery but since no further steps were taken for several months apart from Mr. Tolly's refusal to pay further instalments, repudiation was not allowed. The same result is even more likely where payments are continued; *Jackson* v. *Chrysler*, 1978. If the plaintiff seeks to *rescind for misrepresentation*, above, almost anything other than trial use of the goods may debar him from doing so; *Long* v. *Lloyd*, 1958. On balance then most recent cases on the right to repudiate seem fairly to recognise the realities of the situation, but the position is undeniably unsatisfactory.

CHAPTER TWO

DEFECTIVE GOODS—BUYERS' RIGHTS

Express and Implied Terms

This chapter is concerned with contractual standards of fitness and safety of goods, laid down either by the express terms of a contract of sale or hire purchase or by implication of law. As regards terms expressly agreed between the parties we need not add greatly to what we said in Chapter One. We pointed out there that what is promised will depend very largely on each side's bargaining power, but that if a promise is then broken (for any reason other than impossibility or complete impracticability) the innocent party is entitled as appropriate to repudiate or claim damages, unless the contract itself expressly and lawfully denies him such rights—as to which see Chapter Five.

These are, however, matters decided ultimately by the parties' own words and deeds. The more important questions of law to which we now turn are those concerning standards of fitness and safety which apply *in the absence* of express agreement. The standards which have the widest application are the conditions and warranties implied by sections 12–15 of the Sale of Goods Act, 1893, as amended by the Supply of Goods (Implied Terms) Act, 1973. With appropriate changes in wording these provisions apply also to hire purchase transactions (Schedule 4 of the Consumer Credit Act, 1974), and redemption of trading stamps (section 16 of the 1973 Act). Premium offers or free gifts are not within the Act.

Title

Section 12 says it is an implied condition of a contract of sale that the seller has a right to sell the goods and that there are implied warranties of freedom from any prior rights over the goods and of "quiet possession" of them except in so far as limitations on title are disclosed before sale. This section is not often invoked in a consumer context, but the case of *Rowland* v. *Divall*, 1923, indicates its importance. Here a stolen car was sold to an innocent buyer, B, who resold it to another, C, who bought in equal good faith. When several months later the true owner recovered the car from C it was held that C was entitled to recover from B all he had paid for the car and was not obliged to make any allowance for its use. A good title was fundamental to the contract and so in effect C had received nothing for his money. B therefore had to pay twice for the car he bought from the thief. But if the goods B sold to C were consumables which C then consumed it would seem difficult still to argue that C had received nothing! Section 27 of the Hire Purchase Act, 1964, provides an important exception to the basic rule that the true owner can recover goods sold without his consent. In the case of a motor vehicle sold in breach of a hire purchase agreement it allows the title to pass to a private purchaser acting in good faith. Other limited exceptions to the owner's rights are in sections 21–26 of the Sale of Goods Act.

Description

Section 13 lays down an implied condition that goods sold by description must correspond with that description, and that in sales by both sample and description each must be complied with. The rule applies equally whether the seller describes his goods or whether they "describe themselves"—as shirts, shoes, etc.—on display shelves in front of the buyer. But not everything said about goods is part of their description. This section concerns only the "essence" of the goods—how they might be identified say on a bill or receipt; *Taylor* v. *Combined Buyers*, 1924 (N.Z.). So "newness," for example, might very well be part of a description, expressly or by implication, but "good condition" probably would not. Even so, the precise meaning of "new" is open to argument. In *Phillips* v. *Cycle Finance Corp.*, 1977, for instance, a motor cycle bought as new was actually five years old. The court held that there was no breach of section 13 because the machine had not been driven before nor sold by retail—surely a quite incorrect standard in the circumstances.

If goods do not work properly that of itself does not prove a breach of section 13, as long as they are still basically what was ordered. Such cases would be argued under section 14, below. But if a statement or requirement is indeed part of the description it may be very strictly interpreted and applied. So in *Arcos* v. *Ronnaasen*, 1933, where one-half inch staves were ordered but nine-sixteenth inch staves delivered, the buyer was entitled to reject the goods for breach of condition although they were in fact still suitable for their intended use. This approach is obviously open to abuse. It may give a buyer who has changed his mind about the wisdom of his purchase, perhaps because he intended to resell but now finds the price has fallen, a gratuitous and quite unnecessary chance to back out. In more recent decisions the courts have preferred to ask simply whether the seller's deviation from the contract was of any real significance and if not will refuse to allow the buyer to reject; *Cehave* v. *Bremer* 1975; *Reardon Smith* v. *Hansen Tangen*, 1976. Another point is that the more closely the buyer examines the goods before purchase the less likely they are to be sold by their description. In effect they are then sold "as seen." But an examination of goods only defeats the section if and in so far as it is aimed at and ought to have revealed the kind of shortfall or defect in question; *Beale* v. *Taylor*, 1967.

Merchantable Quality

In practice it is not section 13 but the next one which gives the greatest degree of protection to the consumer and which is most often invoked in the courts. Section 14 is so important that we should note the exact wording of its main provisions, as amended by the Act of 1973 (emphasis added):

"14 (1) Except as provided by this section, and section 15 of this Act and subject to the provision of any other enactment, there is no implied condition or warranty as to the quality or fitness for any particular purpose of goods supplied under a contract of sale.

(2) Where the seller sells goods in the course of a business, there is an implied condition that the goods supplied under the contract are of *merchantable quality*, except that there is no such condition—

(a) as regards defects specifically drawn to the buyer's attention before the contract is made; or

(b) if the buyer examines the goods before the contract is made, as regards defects which that examination ought to reveal.

18

(3) Where the seller sells goods in the course of a business and the buyer, expressly or by implication, makes known to the seller any particular purpose for which the goods are being bought, there is an implied condition that the goods supplied under the contract are *reasonably fit* for that purpose, whether or not that is a purpose for which such goods are commonly supplied, except where the circumstances show that the buyer does not rely, or that it is unreasonable for him to rely, on the seller's skill or judgment."

It will be seen that the section states first the fundamental "caveat emptor" or "buyer beware" principle—*i.e.* that the law sets no minimum standards of fitness of goods except in the circumstances covered by section 14 (2) and (3). But the terms of section 14 are broad, only excluding sales between private individuals—where it is accordingly essential for the buyer to protect himself by persuading the seller to give express promises of fitness. In business sales on the other hand the buyer is given very considerable protection by this section, and since the seller can no longer avoid his liabilities as he once could (Chapter Five) the end result is that the "buyer beware" principle is only a shadow of its former self. Indeed within the limits we shall describe we could say that the burden of responsibility has now moved to the seller—making the rule much more nearly "seller beware." That is not to say of course that the buyer is free to change his mind about what he wants after he has bought the goods, or that the seller must offer other goods or money back if for instance the colour of the goods is not as attractive as the buyer thought it was, or if shoes which seemed to fit him start to pinch. The seller's basic obligations are defined in section 14 in terms of merchantability and reasonable fitness for purpose, which are objective standards rather than personal preferences. They are also conditions, so that in legal theory any breach, however trivial, justifies the buyer in rejecting the goods unless he has already accepted them; sections 11 and 35; Chapter One.

Course of Business

Before we consider the precise meaning of merchantability and reasonable fitness, we should note that each standard applies subject to certain reservations, the first of which, common to both, is that the sale must be made in the course of business. The seller is therefore answerable not only for the fitness of his stock in trade but for other entirely different sorts of goods sold from time to time on a "one off" basis, *e.g.* used scales, display cabinets, delivery vans, and the like, subject to the question of "reliance," below.

Known Defects

Section 14 (2) contains the necessary proviso that a seller is not responsible for defects pointed out to the buyer before sale, nor for those the buyer ought to have seen in any examination he may have made of the goods. There is no obligation as such upon the buyer to examine goods before purchase.

Merchantability

The vital question is of course as to the meaning of the phrase "merchantable quality." Basically it must mean "saleable"—but as what, and to whom? The answer cannot depend on one particular buyer's likes and dislikes. If he chooses to reject goods anyone else would find acceptable, they are clearly still merchantable. And they could still be so despite faults which prevented the buyer from using them as he intended but which nevertheless left them usable for some totally different purpose; *Kendall* v. *Lillico*, 1968—groundnut meal unsuitable for its intended purpose as poultry food, but still usable as animal feeding stuff—House of Lords held the goods merchantable, and said they would not be so only if "in the form in which they were tendered they were of *no use for any purpose* (emphasis added) for which goods which complied with the description under which these goods were sold would normally be used, and hence were not saleable under that description." This undoubtedly sets a very low standard which while perhaps justifiable on the facts of *Kendall* could scarcely be applied in every case, least of all where the prices of higher and lower qualities differ significantly; *Brown* v. *Craiks*, 1970.

A further complication arises when the faults in the goods are not visible on delivery but only appear later. How should the buyer's rights be decided in this event? Judges have said that "The goods should be in such a state that a buyer, fully acquainted with the facts and therefore knowing what hidden defects exist and not being limited to their apparent condition, would buy them without abatement of the price"; *Grant* v. *Australian Knitting Mills*, 1933. But since no one in his right mind would buy goods at the normal price if he knew they were defective, this test seems unrealistic and it creates certain other problems, as mentioned below. No reference is made to it in the definition of merchantability enacted in 1973 to try to resolve these various doubts, though the purpose of the Supply of Goods (Amendment) Bill, introduced in 1979, was to give this test statutory recognition.

The definition adopted in section 7 of the Supply of Goods (Implied Terms) Act, 1973, amending section 62 of the Sale of Goods Act, is as follows: "Goods of any kind are of merchantable quality within the meaning of this Act if they are as fit for the purpose or purposes for which goods of that kind are commonly bought as it is reasonable to expect having regard to any description applied to them, the price (if relevant) and all the other relevant circumstances."

It must be admitted that this provision does not take us very much further, particularly since it defines merchantability in terms of reasonable fitness—the requirement in section 14 (3), itself undefined. Indeed all we have established so far is that the standard of merchantability is both inherently imprecise and absolutely essential! Everything depends, as lawyers so often have to say, upon the facts of the particular case. That being so, let us now look at some more specific problems and examples which may perhaps give us a clearer idea of what is involved. Our task is made no easier by the fact that most reported cases concern transactions between businesses and tell us very little about the rights of consumers as such.

We should observe first that although the requirements of merchantable quality and reasonable fitness overlap they are still quite separate and distinct. When a customer orders a new car or a washing machine, for instance, he expects not only that it will work properly—*i.e.* be reasonably fit for its purpose—but also that it is not delivered in a chipped or damaged or discoloured state. If it were delivered in this condition he would no doubt either refuse to accept it despite its mechanical fitness, or at least demand a reduction in price. Most sellers would likewise treat such goods as shop soiled, and offer them at a lower price. To the extent that the goods would not be bought or sold as "new" they are evidently not merchantable as such. It is convenient therefore to look at problems of appearance and similar superficial or minor faults under the heading of merchantability, and then discuss more serious mechanical or other fundamental defects in relation to reasonable fitness.

Three cases may usefully be compared. In *Jackson* v. *Rotax*, 1910, the buyer was held entitled to reject a consignment of motor horns, 10 per cent. of which were found scratched or dented on delivery. In the New Zealand case of *Winsley* v. *Woodfield*, 1929, the buyer's right to reject a £90 woodworking machine was upheld because it was supplied with a defective guard costing £1 to put right. And in the Canadian case of *I.B.M.* v. *Shcherban*, 1925, the buyer successfully rejected a $300 computer scale because of a broken dial glass—although this fault did not affect the operation of the machine and would have cost only 30 cents to repair. The decision in *Jackson* is hardly surprising in view of the extent of the damage, but what if only 1 or 2 per cent. of the horns had been faulty? The court might well have said the buyer had got essentially what he asked for, and so had to pay the full price. But the two Commonwealth decisions indicate that the standard of acceptability could sometimes be much higher than we have so far suggested. The element of danger was of course relevant in *Winsley*, but the I.B.M. case strongly and unambiguously supports the view that finish or appearance can be most important for its own sake—though the case was no doubt very much on the borderline. Even the fussiest of customers must admit that perfection is impossible, and sooner or later the judge would have to apply the ancient maxim "de minimis non curat lex"—"the law ignores trivialities"—and reject the buyer's claim. He would often be right to do so, for example with regard to goods supplied for industrial use where finish or appearance is rarely vital. But we could surely say that in consumer transactions different considerations now apply. The whole burden of advertising of consumer goods is upon their immaculate appearance or packaging. The consumer's expectations are raised accordingly, and he will not and should not need to accept goods which are plainly substandard in this respect. The effect of section 14 (2) in other words seems to be (though we cannot say categorically that it is) to enable a buyer of consumer goods to reject them for relatively minor and purely cosmetic blemishes. This may seem a somewhat extreme remedy, but that is the "all or nothing" problem arising out of the Act's classification of remedies.

Is the buyer's position affected if such minor faults are not noticed at the time of sale or delivery, but only become apparent after use? We mentioned earlier the difficulty posed by the rule in *Grant* v. *A.K.M.*, to the effect that the buyer's rights should be based on his assumed knowledge of faults hidden from him at the time of sale. Apart from the difficulty that he would not have bought the goods in the first place, it seems unreasonable to let a buyer who has actually used the goods reject them because of some trivial flaw he has only just found—even though he might properly have rejected them on delivery for exactly the same reason. Common sense suggests that at this stage he must simply make the best of his bargain.

Ultimately then merchantability seems to be decided by the response of the reasonable buyer; *Cehave* v. *Bremer*, 1977. The Molony Report on Consumer Protection (1962) put it this way: "It has been suggested that the term 'unmerchantable' is inapt to describe the sort of defect encountered with mechanical or electrical goods when all that is required is some small adjustment by an expert. We are not disposed to agree. If an appliance does not work, or only works imperfectly or intermittently, it is small consolation to the purchaser to know that an expert can readily put it right. He is entitled to an article in such condition that *a reasonable man acting reasonably would accept it* (Author's italics). If the article falls below that standard, whatever the cause, he has just complaint about its merchantability. It is true that the Courts have not had much opportunity to develop a theory of what constitutes 'unmerchantability' in this type of article. We do not doubt that they would find it well within their competence to do so."

If this is indeed the test it is undeniably still a very broad one, but it does take due account of the type and value of the goods—consumer or industrial—and of the time the defects were discovered. It indicates also that the task of the law is twofold; both to discourage shoddy workmanship and to prevent buyers from behaving unreasonably. It would probably be unwise as well as extremely difficult to lay down any more precise standard.

Reasonable Fitness for Purpose

The second and perhaps still more important implied condition is that laid down by section 14 (3) of the Sale of Goods Act as

23

re-phrased by section 3 of the Supply of Goods (Implied Terms) Act:

> "Where the seller sells goods in the course of a business and the buyer, expressly or by implication, makes known to the seller any particular purpose for which the goods are being bought, there is an implied condition that the goods supplied under the contract are reasonably fit for that purpose, whether or not that is a purpose for which such goods are commonly supplied, except where the circumstances show that the buyer does not rely, or that it is unreasonable for him to rely, on the seller's skill or judgment."

Purpose

The condition of reasonable fitness applies only within certain limits. As we noted earlier, the sale must be in the course of business whether or not the goods are of a kind normally sold in that business. The condition will not be implied unless the purpose the goods are wanted for is known to the seller, and only if the buyer relies on the seller's skill or judgment. These requirements do not often present any great difficulty. The uses of most goods are obvious—clothes for wearing, cars for driving about in, and so on—and so the buyer only has to tell the seller why he wants them if he has some unusual purpose in mind, such as exceptionally heavy or prolonged use. *Griffiths* v. *Conway*, 1939, is an example of the consequences of failure to disclose a special requirement. The plaintiff bought a tweed coat without mentioning her allergy to certain materials. The seller was not liable for the resulting rash because the coat was perfectly suitable for anyone else. And the mere fact that the seller *is* aware that some special use is intended does not *of itself* make him liable for any inadequacies; *Teheran Europe Co.* v. *Belton*, 1968—seller knew goods intended for export—they were not usable where exported but reasonably fit in all other respects—no liability.

Reliance

Reliance on the seller's skill and judgment does not normally have to be proved. "A buyer goes to the shops in the confidence that the tradesman has selected his stock with skill and judgment"; *Grant* v. *A.K.M.*, above. This may still be so where the buyer takes his own plan or specification to the seller so that he can produce the finished article for him, if and insofar as the seller holds himself out as expert in the production of such goods—*Ashington Piggeries* v. *Hill*, 1972—unless perhaps the buyer's design is altogether novel and experimental. There may be no reliance either where it is the *buyer's* job to handle or look after the goods in a certain way, and his failure to do this which creates the danger or defect. In *Heil* v. *Hedges*, 1951, a customer bought some pork chops from a butcher. They were infected with worms. The customer did not cook the meat properly, and contracted trichinosis. Her subsequent claim against the butcher was unsuccessful, since this was the kind of risk which could be expected if meat were not cooked properly. Or again there would be no reliance if on the facts the buyer were more of an expert than the seller but failed to check the suitability of the goods for his own specialised purpose: *Teheran Europe Co.*, above; *Feast* v. *Vincent*, 1974 (N.Z.). Similarly if before purchase the goods are comprehensively examined by the buyer or his expert adviser, he is evidently relying on his own or his adviser's skill rather than the seller's; *McDonald* v. *Empire Garage*, 1975. This latter case seems very unfair in that the seller of a car escaped liability on these grounds despite the fact that no examination could possibly have revealed the design fault which eventually caused a brake failure.

Reasonable Fitness

As with "merchantable quality" there is no final definition of this crucial phrase. "Reasonableness" is clearly a compromise standard; a requirement falling some way short of perfection. If a higher standard is required it must be expressly asked for. We might say to begin with that goods are reasonably fit if they do "more or less" what is required of them—if they are simply "usable." But even if we put the rule like this we can see immediately that its practical effects must differ according to the functions and complexity of the goods in question. An electric light bulb for example must work the moment it is switched on, or not at all (—though its life span may not necessarily be the same as every other bulb). With multi-functional and much more complex goods such as motor cars, on the other hand, a much greater degree of tolerance or imperfection might reasonably be expected. The consumer's expectation must depend also on whether the goods are new or secondhand and on whether they are expensive and supposed to be of good quality or are cheap and so probably less reliable or durable. If one buys a new Rolls Royce it surely cannot be a sufficient compliance with the law that it "goes," but nothing more.

There are, however, surprisingly few cases to illustrate these propositions, and fewer still about consumer goods. We shall concentrate here upon the handful of cases on new and second-hand motor vehicles, representing as they do the biggest single investment most consumers make in goods. The case of *Farnworth Finance* v. *Attryde*, 1970, concerned a new Enfield motor cycle which had to be returned twice to the suppliers and once to the manufacturers for various lethal defects—including headlight, brake and chain failures—to be remedied. After four months of such difficulties Mr. Attryde sought to return the machine and recover his money. He succeeded, despite the length of time he had had and used the vehicle. Lord Denning said that the implied condition of fitness meant that it had to be roadworthy and safe, which it clearly was not.

The decision is obviously right and necessary, but tells us nothing about consumers' rights where the problem is not that of danger to life or limb but the much more common one of poor quality or performance. *Millar* v. *Turpie*, 1976, is an interesting Scottish case which makes it clear that a buyer cannot reject a car because of one small, easily remediable and not particularly dangerous fault such as an oil leak from the power assisted steering unit. But what if there are lots of faults and continuing loss of use? In *Spencer* v. *Rye*, 1972, the plaintiff bought a new Triumph Vitesse. The next day the throttle cable broke and the car had to be towed back to the dealer's. It was returned to them 12 times in the following three months for assorted other defects to be dealt with, including roof leaks, loss of oil, a door which needed to be rehung and in particular the problem of the radiator overheating every 100 miles. The judge agreed that a car which would not go more than 100 miles at a time was useless, which is undeniable, but his comments on all the other faults are most significant: "[They] may have been very irritating, but all were eventually cured and *did not amount to sufficient reason for him to reject the car*" (Emphasis added). A car must of course be accepted as reasonably fit if it goes satisfactorily, if not perfectly. Teething troubles of some sort are inevitable. But when a new car develops several "very irritating" faults like those listed and has to go back to the dealer a dozen times with all the consequential loss and inconvenience to the owner, one might think it so unsatisfactory as to be intolerable. The judge in *Spencer* evidently did not think so, and if that is indeed the law it must be said it accepts depressingly and unnecessarily low standards of workmanship and performance. A law which requires of a new car only that it is basically "roadworthy"—in the limited sense that it starts and stops and goes safely—simply does not meet the expectations of the buyer. If that were all he wanted he might just as well buy a second-hand model. Would the judge have reached the same decision in relation to a product such as a washing machine, where day-to-day efficiency and availability are considerations at least as important as safety?

Support for the application of a higher standard comes from a number of Canadian cases. In *Lightburn* v. *Belmont Sales*, 1969, the plaintiff bought a new Cortina, which he had been promised would meet his needs as to economy and reliability but which he found as the judge put it he could not rely on "from one hour to the next." The car had to be towed back to the dealer's twice and was returned there nearly 20 times in the eight months following sale because of continuous trouble with the electrical system. The judge ordered the defendants to take the car back and return the purchase price to the plaintiff, and laid down a standard of fitness apparently in advance of that required in England. "I conclude that the defendant was in breach of a fundamental term of the contract to purchase a motor car of workable character capable of giving a *sustained reliable performance throughout the year.*" [Author's italics.]

The facts in *Gibbons* v. *Trapp Motors*, 1970, were very similar. "The plaintiff purchased a new automobile [a Pontiac convertible] and by no means a low cost one and was entitled to enjoy from it a performance typical of a new car from an established manufacturer. Instead of such a performance he in fact acquired a running fight with a chronically defective car." Over 30 hours' repair time was required in the first 10 months, followed by a period of 10 days during which the car was to be brought once and for all to reasonable running order. But even that lengthy treatment failed to deal with its many weaknesses in "steering and roadability [and] reliability." The judge held that all these various defects together constituted a breach of condition.

Although the question was partly one of safety it seems clear that repeated loss of use and unreliability were again the main factors. "Such use was not free from justified worries on his part, inconveniences and restrictions in what I choose to term serene possession of a reliably performing car"—a strikingly apt and agreeable phrase indicating again a higher standard than that in *Spencer* or *Farnworth Finance*. His Honour held that the fact that the defendant had tried to repair all the defects at his own expense did not compel the plaintiff to accept the car(—a view reinforced in *Friskin* v. *Holiday Chevrolet–Oldsmobile*, 1977, another Canadian case, where it was said that a seller cannot insist upon the buyer giving him the opportunity to repair. He can, however, reasonably expect the chance to confirm whether the goods are or are not fit; *Millar* v. *Turpie*, above). The judgment in *Gibbons* was accordingly that the dealer should take back the car and return the purchase price less half the plaintiff's cost of hiring replacement vehicles. A still more recent example where persistent starting trouble was held to justify repudiation was *Finlay* v. *Metro-Toyota*, 1978. On the basis of all these Canadian cases it is again suggested that the proper test of the fitness of goods is whether they should be *satisfactory as such for a reasonable buyer*. Whether that would be accepted as the law in England or whether the question would be as we put it above "do the goods 'more or less' fulfil their purpose?" remains unresolved.

With regard to second-hand goods a comparison between the cases of *Bartlett* v. *Marcus*, 1965, and *Crowther* v. *Shannon Motor Co.*, 1975, is instructive. *Bartlett* concerned a used Jaguar car sold for £950. The dealer warned the buyer that minor clutch repairs might be necessary. Within a few weeks clutch defects developed costing £45 to remedy. The buyer claimed damages for that amount on the ground that the car was not reasonably fit for its purpose. He lost his claim because in the court's view this was the kind of repair and level of cost to be expected in the circumstances. In *Crowther* another Jaguar which had done 80,000 miles was sold for £390. A month later the engine seized up completely and had to be renewed, for a further £400 or so. The dealers argued that this was the same sort of case as *Bartlett*, but the court thought not. Evidence was given that Jaguar engines were supposed to run for at least 100,000 miles, so that the buyer had got very much less than he expected, and in any event a completely useless engine was rather more serious than a clutch defect. The buyer's rights in such cases therefore depend entirely on matters of fact and degree. We have to leave unanswered various further questions of life-span, availability of spare parts and the like which are all undoubtedly aspects of reasonable fitness, again turning on matters of fact and degree, on which English law has little or nothing to say.

We end this section with the thought that while these decisions on second-hand goods seem eminently sensible it is disappointing to find that in England at least no perceptibly higher standard seems to have been set for new goods. Perhaps one day soon someone (preferably someone else!) will have the courage and resources to take a complaint about shoddy goods to court and be rewarded with a judgment which recognises the need both to clarify the law and to uphold the reasonable expectations of the consumer. And by way of postscript we might note too the Commonwealth view that the consumer is so much at risk in the second-hand car market in particular that he should be given some more specific form of protection than that provided by the Sale of Goods Act (and apart from the criminal law). In Canada, Australia and New Zealand car dealers must now be licensed, and their overall standards of commercial behaviour are therefore subject to the periodic scrutiny of an independent agency. In Canada certain Provinces require the dealer to give a certificate of fitness before sale. The certificate is in a prescribed form, listing parts of the vehicle which must have been checked by the dealer and found satisfactory. It may be regarded as an obligatory express warranty. Recent Australian and New Zealand statutes require that used cars sold in various stipulated price ranges should carry either express warranties of so many months or miles, or a "notice of declared defects," together with the estimated cost of remedying the defects. The dealer may be liable for the cost of repairs in excess of the estimate and for any defects not listed. Thus a buyer who sees an inexpensive car to which the dealer is not prepared to attach a warranty can decide for himself whether it is worth the extra cost which he knows will be necessary. Britain has no equivalent of any of these measures.

Strict Liability

The cases we have looked at show that if the goods in question are not merchantable or reasonably fit for their purpose *the retailer is liable whether or not he knew or could have known of the defects, and whether or not it was within his power to remedy them*. This conclusion is inescapable if one looks at the wording of section 14. It says that goods sold in the course of business *must be reasonably fit*, not that the seller must do his best to see that they are fit. How, or why, goods fall short of this standard is of no concern to the customer. Apart from the car cases another impressive example of this truism is *Frost* v. *Aylesbury Dairy*, 1905, where the dairy sold milk containing typhoid germs which could not at that time have been discovered by any reasonable inspection it could have undertaken. The dairy was none the less liable to the buyer for the illness he suffered. It is in other words the *retailer* who is primarily responsible for the fitness of the goods he sells, and not the manufacturer. We shall examine the different liabilities the manufacturer faces in Chapter Four.

This short but vital point on retailers' liability is fundamental to sales law, but it is still surprisingly little known—either in industry or commerce or among members of the general public. Its value to the consumer, however, cannot be overstated. He knows where the goods came from—the shop in the High Street—and he can be reasonably sure that if he makes a fuss there he will probably get redress of some sort. In particular, the shop in the High Street is usually vulnerable and responsive to the threat of bad publicity which would result from legal action against it. A buyer who sends his goods back to the manufacturer in reliance on his guarantee may gain satisfaction that way, but he runs the risk of losing his simplest and most direct remedy. It is important to note, however, that the position is different in hire-purchase transactions, as explained below.

Retailers might not see the value or fairness of strict liability quite as clearly as consumers. Faults in pre-packed goods are none of their doing and it might seem most unfair that they should have to foot the bill. The fact remains that retailers make their living out of selling the goods in question and should therefore accept some responsibility for them. And if the fault is indeed that of someone else in the chain of distribution the retailer can sue back up the line under the same section of the same Act (subject to the existence of any exclusion clauses en route and the effect on them of the Unfair Contract Terms Act; Chapter Five).

The last implied conditions are in section 15, which governs sales by sample. The bulk must correspond with the sample, the buyer must be able to compare bulk and sample, and the goods must be free of hidden defects rendering them unmerchantable. Sales by sample are relatively rare as between retailers and consumers except perhaps as regards items such as cloth or carpet or wine. If the consumer says "I want a vacuum cleaner like that one over there" he does not thereby bring the sale within the terms of this section.

Repudiation or Damages?

Now we have examined the seller's express and implied duties the question arises as to the buyer's remedies if they are broken. We noted in Chapter One the vital distinctions between conditions and warranties and the rules on "acceptance." At this point therefore we must refer the consumer who believes he can establish a breach of condition against the retailer to p. 14 so that he may see there whether he is still able to repudiate or can only claim damages in accordance with the principles discussed on pages 11–15.

Hire Purchase

English law sees hire purchase contracts as essentially different from contracts of sale, particularly with regard to the transfer of rights of ownership. In the law's view there is only a contract to hire, and an option to purchase by the last instalment. Even in so-called conditional sales the rights of ownership are not transferred immediately as they are in most sales, but only on payment of all instalments. It is also a feature of many hire-purchase transactions that the credit—the "time to pay"—is provided not by the dealer but by a third party, a finance house. The dealer is really only a middleman, who makes the goods available and provides the forms and facilities which enable the consumer to hire the goods from the finance house, and then drops out of the transaction. That in turn means that in hire-purchase transactions the implied conditions as to title, description, merchantable quality, reasonable fitness and correspondence with sample, which are otherwise the same as those in the Sale of Goods Act, are imposed upon the finance house and not upon the dealer; sections 8–11, Supply of Goods (Implied Terms) Act, 1973, amended by Schedule 4, Consumer Credit Act, 1974. This is of course much less satisfactory from the consumer's point of view, for the very reason that the finance house is probably not locally based and may be correspondingly less responsive to pressure.

It follows that in hire-purchase transactions the dealer could only be personally liable for defective goods in very limited circumstances, *e.g.* if he made an express promise as to their fitness to the consumer, for which the consumer gave consideration (see Chapter One) by entering into a hire-purchase agreement. In *Andrews* v. *Hopkinson*, 1957, for example, a used-car dealer promised a prospective hire-purchase customer that the car was "a good little bus" and that he "would stake [his] life upon it." Unfortunately he staked the customer's life on it instead, and was liable for damages for breach of contract. He was also liable for negligence since on the facts he should have known the car was unsafe. A dealer would be liable too for any misrepresentation he might make which fell short of a term of the contract; Chapter One. Whether or not the finance house is itself the owner of the goods, it is liable for the dealer's breach of contract or any misrepresentation made by him in the course of negotiations, unless the cash price of the goods is under £30 or over £10,000; sections 56 and 75, Consumer Credit Act. The same two sections apply to credit card companies except when credit must be repaid in one instalment as with Diners' Club and American Express cards; Consumer Credit (Exempt Agreements) Order, 1977.

Conclusion

It will be remembered that all the rules and remedies we have discussed so far are those of the civil law. Some but not all of these issues are also regulated by the criminal law, notably questions of deceptive advertising and certain matters of safety of food and other goods. The circumstances in which the consumer has a right to complain to an appropriate enforcement agency and leave the agency to take action on his behalf are set out in Chapter Six. If the problem is purely civil the consumer may need advice and assistance in taking legal action himself, and the availability of such assistance is described in Chapter Seven.

CHAPTER THREE

DEFECTIVE SERVICES

The liabilities of suppliers of services, like those of suppliers of goods (Chapter Two), may be defined either by the express terms of the contract between supplier and customer or by terms added to the contract by law—or, if there is no contract, by the duty to take reasonable care discussed in Chapter Four. The present chapter is concerned with the contractual position only. Where the contract specifies the required services in detail it should be relatively easy for the judge to say whether or not they have been supplied—but even here there may be room for doubt. As we said in Chapter One, the words used by the parties may sometimes be open to very different interpretations. We should also note that whether or not a breach of contract or negligence can be proved against the supplier he may be criminally liable under the Trade Descriptions Act or other legislation against misleading advertising; Chapter Six.

Express Terms

Building, Decorating and Repair Work

Disputes quite often occur as to whether building or similar work has been done in compliance with contract terms. Each case turns of course on its own merits—*i.e.* on what the contract requires and what work has in fact been done—but some of the cases raise points of more general interest about the customer's remedies for breach of contract. We noted in Chapter One the possible remedies of repudiation and/or damages, and said that in "entire" contracts quite small deficiencies might justify repudiation unless the contract has been "substantially performed." The question is really whether a contractor should be awarded part of his fee if he has done only part of the job, or, since the agreement was that he be paid for doing the job properly, should get nothing if it is done badly.

Examples include *Bolton* v. *Mahadeva*, 1972, where it was held that a householder need not pay anything to a contractor who had promised to instal central heating for £560 but whose workmanship was so bad that the system could not be used and cost £174 to put right. But in *Kiely* v. *Medcraft*, 1965, where a contract to paint a house for £520 was badly executed and remedial work would have cost £200, the owner still had to pay £320, presumably on the basis that he had got something rather than nothing—a doubtful decision. Failure to provide the promised regular repair service for goods which were in any case clearly defective was held to justify both annulment of the contract for the future and cancellation of all arrears in *Ditchburn* v. *Crich*, 1966.

Holidays

Disappointed holiday expectations are another quite common source of complaint, but of course the holidaymaker has to prove something more than a difference of opinion if he wants compensation. The difficulty was illustrated in *Sandbanks Hotel* v. *Wallman*, 1962, a dispute over the proper size of a "double room"—which the hotel guest lost. Examples of "legitimate" grievances include *Jarvis* v. *Swans Tours*, 1963, and *Jackson* v. *Horizon Holidays*, 1975. The brochures and agencies in question expressly promised various specific attractions which were not forthcoming, and there were other disappointments in the way of poor food and dirty facilities, so that the holidays were really completely ruined. In *Jarvis* the damages were approximately double the original cost of the holiday—for, in effect, loss of the plaintiff's only fortnight's holiday in the year—while in *Jackson*, where the family at least enjoyed the services of another hotel during the holiday, the original costs were reimbursed.

The "Miscellaneous Statutory Provisions" noted at the end of this chapter include protection against travel agencies' insolvency.

Implied Terms

If the parties to a contract of sale or hire-purchase of goods do not say exactly what standards of fitness they want they can always turn to the Sale of Goods Act or Consumer Credit Act for guidance. But as far as contracts for *services* are concerned it has been left almost entirely to the judges in each particular case to decide what minimum standards should apply. The distinction between goods and services is important both for this reason and because liability for defective services can still be excluded more easily than for goods; Chapter Five. They are not of course clear or watertight distinctions. Contracts to repair cars or instal goods or apply hair dyes, for example, have been held to be for work and materials—*i.e.* services—even though part of the price is clearly for goods. But a contract to provide a meal or make a suit is for goods, and so within the Sale of Goods Act.

We said in Chapter One that the judges would not imply terms in contracts unless it was actually essential to do so to give the contract any meaning. Whether any and if so what term will be implied therefore depends very much on the problems posed by the contract in question. But terms such as the following are likely to be implied failing express agreement between the parties.

Reasonable Time
Unless a definite period is fixed by the contract the judges will imply a term that services must be completed within a reasonable time; *Charnock* v. *Liverpool Corporation*, 1968—car repairs estimated to take five weeks still not finished after eight weeks—breach of contract: *Stanners* v. *High Wycombe Borough Council*, 1968—liability for not completing demolition work as quickly as possible and so leaving adjacent premises open to theft. Suppliers' delays nonetheless remain a common source of worry and difficulty for consumers. If goods are sent back to the seller or manufacturer for repair, for example, the consumer probably has no idea how long the work will take and almost certainly does not know of any way of getting the work done with reasonable speed. If he were to threaten legal action—an unlikely event—the article might well simply be returned to him in the same defective state. And if he were actually to claim damages for delay he could be in considerable difficulty in showing what loss he had suffered. Codes of business conduct sponsored by the Office of Fair Trading, Chapter Six, may have a useful part to play here, emphasising as some of them do the virtues of prompt service.

Reasonable Price

If the price of services is not fixed beforehand the customer will have to pay a reasonable price for them once they are supplied. The judge decides what is reasonable in the light of prevailing charges for that kind of work (or in the case of solicitors and other professional men's fees the amount may be challenged before the appropriate professional body). But if the price is only in doubt because the customer did not trouble to inquire about it at the outset it seems he must pay whatever the supplier asks. The supplier is under no duty as such to keep the price down by using the cheapest methods or materials. Prices for decorating and building work and the like may be very difficult to assess in advance. If they are given as estimates or quotations they may still be binding upon the supplier, depending on the wording used; *Croshaw* v. *Pritchard*, 1889. Once a price is agreed it cannot be increased because of, *e.g.* extra costs to the supplier, unless there is a "rise and fall" or other such clause allowing for variation or the buyer accepts the new rate; *North Ocean Shipping* v. *Hyundai*, 1978. Under the Estate Agents Act, 1979, agents must give particulars of their charges before any contract is made, or varied.

Business Efficacy

Generally the court will be willing to imply any appropriate term necessary to stop the contract from being completely nullified; *The Moorcock*, 1889. As emphasised in Chapter One, however, the test is that of *necessity*; the business efficacy rule certainly does not mean that every disadvantageous bargain will be remedied. But if, for example, a car is to be sold the logbook must be available or else there is no contract—*Bentworth Finance* v. *Lubert*, 1968—and goods must be delivered in the same condition as when ordered, subject to any inevitable deterioration; *Financings* v. *Stimson*, 1962. If a contract provides for termination "on notice," or makes no provision for notice at all, business efficacy requires a period of reasonable notice to be determined; *Staffordshire A.H.A.* v. *S. Staffordshire Waterworks*, 1978.

Reasonable Fitness

Perhaps the most important question is the standard of fitness of services required by the law—but unfortunately the rules are not at all clearly established. In contracts of carriage or storage ("bailment") the carrier or "bailee" is obliged only to take reasonable care of the goods unless the contract specifies a higher duty, and subject also to any contractual right to delegate this duty and to the operation of any valid exclusion clause (Chapter Five); *Houghland* v. *Low*, 1962—liability of coach company for luggage lost through lack of supervision. The duty of care is the same whether or not there is a contract or payment; *Mitchell* v. *Ealing L.B.C.*, 1978. But merely leaving goods on another's land, *e.g.* a car in a car park, does not of itself create a bailment; *Ashby* v. *Tolhurst*, 1937. This case contrasts with *Manitoba Insurance* v. *Midway Chrysler*, 1978 (Can.), where a garage keeping a car on its premises overnight for repairs was held liable for an employee's negligence in leaving the key in the car, as a result of which it was stolen.

Under contracts to provide work or materials the duty seems to be higher. As with goods the work *must be reasonably fit for its purpose*, and it is not enough for the supplier to show he has done his best, or could not have found or prevented the faults in his work, if it is in fact unsatisfactory. In *Myers* v. *Brent Cross Service*, 1934, a car repairer was held liable for defects in parts supplied, even though he could not have detected the faults himself. Similarly in *Volk* v. *Schreiber*, 1978 (Can.), a travel agent was liable for misinterpreting visa requirements, again without proof of negligence. The cases also suggest that to fulfil his implied duty the supplier's express commitments might have to be quite broadly interpreted. So in *Taylor* v. *Kiddey*, 1968, a car service contract to attend among other matters to the steering was held improperly carried out when the wheels were not inspected and an accident thereby occurred. The wheels were, after all, an integral part of the steering.

We should say again, however, that although the duty is strict it is not a guarantee of perfection. A burglar alarm, for example, might still be reasonably fit for its purpose even though it can be wrenched off the wall and so silenced; *David* v. *Afa-Minerva*, 1974. It should be emphasised too that liability is strict only if there is a contract. A car repairer's liability in contract is owed only to his customer, not to other people in the car who may be injured because of his faulty workmanship; *Sigurdson* v. *Hillcrest Services*, 1977 (Can.). Strict liability might still apply even if the customer nominated his own sub-contractor, but could be displaced if he undertook his own testing of or research into the materials supplied; *Gloucester C.C.* v. *Richardson*, 1968.

The fitness of land and buildings has been the subject of much confusing litigation, and attempts have been made to regulate the position by statute. At common law no contractual term will be implied as to the physical or legal fitness of land or houses sold for occupation or development; *Hill* v. *Harris*, 1965. But if the seller agrees to build or complete a house it must be reasonably fit for occupation, unless that would require him to do something inconsistent with what he had contracted to do; *Lynch* v. *Thorne*, 1956. If injury or damage to property has occurred because of the seller's or builder's or surveyor's negligence there may be a successful claim in tort; *Anns* v. *Merton L.B.C.*, 1977. So far as leases are concerned, there is a term of reasonable fitness of furnished property, but not unfurnished—an obscure distinction; *Wilson* v. *Finch-Hatton*, 1877.

Under section 1 of the Defective Premises Act, 1972, a person who contracts to sell land and build or complete houses upon it is bound to build "in a workmanlike or as the case may be professional manner with proper materials and so that as regards that work the dwelling will be fit for habitation when completed." The duty is strict, *i.e.* it applies whether or not the builder could have detected the faults in his materials, and is owed not only to the purchaser but to "every person who acquires an interest . . . in the building" for six years from the date of completion. This is a very short period and even so would not benefit for example a child in the household injured because of a defective installation within that period—but a claim for negligence might be successful in circumstances not covered by the Act. Legislation on leases includes the Housing Act, 1957, which provides for the fitness of properties of small rateable value, and duties to repair are implied by the Housing Act, 1961.

Professional Services
In deciding how "fit" services ought to be the common law draws a distinction between "professional" and "non-professional" services. In *Greaves* v. *Baynham Meikle*, 1977, which concerned the defective design of a building, professional men were said to include doctors, lawyers, accountants, architects and

engineers—but we cannot of course be sure who else might come within that classification. Its importance is that the standard of care expected of the professional man or woman is lower than that of the non-professional. We have seen that the non-professional supplier must ensure that his services are reasonably fit for their purpose. If he fails he is liable, whether or not he has been negligent. But if he is a professional, his duty is simply to take reasonable care. If his services do not fulfil their purpose he is under no liability unless guilty of negligence. The reason for the distinction may be that the fitness or otherwise of essentially intellectual skills and abilities is more difficult to measure or guarantee than it is where goods and materials and manual work are involved. At all events the surgeon or solicitor is usually sued for negligence rather than for breach of contract. Barristers cannot be sued for negligence in the conduct of a case in court, but like the rest of us may be liable for negligent advice despite the absence of any contractual relationship; *Saif-Ali* v. *Mitchell*, 1978; *Hedley Byrne* v. *Heller*, 1961.

But there are exceptions even to the general rule of professional negligence. Lord Denning pointed out in *Greaves* that "Where a dentist agrees to make a set of false teeth for a patient there is an implied warranty that they will fit his gums"—*i.e.* in this situation the professional worker *is* strictly liable for the success or failure of his work. Perhaps it is all a question of degree, depending on whether the work is done primarily with the brain or primarily with the hands. No clear answer can be given.

Miscellaneous Statutory Provisions

Parliament has made various attempts to control the conditions of entry into certain occupations and so to reduce the possibilities of bad service, or to lessen the worst effects of such service should it occur. Several Acts provide machinery to ensure that only "fit and proper" persons shall provide particular kinds of service. The individuals concerned include doctors, nurses, solicitors and the like, and recently licensing requirements have been introduced for estate agents, employment agencies, individuals or companies providing credit, life insurance companies and insurance brokers. Insurance cover is compulsory for certain occupations, such as solicitors and, since 1979, estate agents. When a professional body exists, *e.g.* the Law Society regulating the conduct of solicitors, complaints should generally be raised with that body first. Claims against solicitors for negligence must still, however, be made through the courts.

Public concern on the collapse of insurance companies led to the Policyholders' Protection Act, 1975. The Act protects persons insured by authorised insurance companies. Where insurance is compulsory, as for employers, the new Policyholders' Protection Board must ensure by means of a levy that the liabilities of insolvent companies are met in full. In the case of compulsory motor insurance, however, the existing agreements between the Ministry of Transport and the Motor Insurers Bureau continue to apply—reaching, with certain limitations, the same results. As regards other general insurance by individuals, *e.g.* life insurance, the Board secures the payment of 90 per cent. of any amount due. Under long term policies where the insured event has not occurred before the company becomes insolvent the Board must try to secure continuity of insurance, with benefits again at a 90 per cent. rate.

Another somewhat similar form of protection has been devised for holidaymakers travelling abroad by air. Most people booking package holidays do so through agencies licensed by the Civil Aviation Authority. Under the Air Travel Reserve Fund Act, 1975, the C.A.A. imposes a levy on licencees to protect holidaymakers in the event of an agency's insolvency.

CHAPTER FOUR

MANUFACTURERS' AND DISTRIBUTORS' LIABILITIES

In previous chapters we discussed the liabilities of a seller of goods or supplier of services to the buyer of those goods or services—in both cases liabilities arising under the express or implied terms of a contract. So far as the manufacturer is concerned however there is usually no contract between him and the buyer or user of the goods, and in English law that fact makes a profound difference to the nature of his liability if the user suffers loss or injury. The position may change before long, as and when European product liability proposals become law. The effect of these proposals is outlined at the end of this chapter.

We have seen that liability under a contract is strict—that come what may (subject to impossibility or impracticability of performance) the parties must fulfil their obligations or be in breach of contract. There is as it were a duty to succeed, not just to try. But if no contract exists then the duty owed by one person to another is seen by English law as correspondingly less strict. The origin of this non-contractual or "tortious" duty is the case of *Donoghue* v. *Stevenson*, 1932, in which the plaintiff drank the contents of an opaque, sealed bottle of ginger beer bought from a retailer by a friend. The bottle contained a decomposed snail, which gave the plaintiff severe gastro-enteritis. Who should she sue? Clearly the only person who could be responsible for the contents of that bottle was the manufacturer. The House of Lords duly held him so (after a monumental struggle to establish what one would think was a painfully simple and obvious point) and thereby established that suppliers of goods and services must take *reasonable care* to ensure that they are safe for the ultimate user. A "user" includes anyone likely to be affected by the goods or services in question, *e.g.* a passer-by injured as a result of a defective car repair.

The practical consequences of these differences between contractual and non-contractual liabilities may be illustrated in this way. Suppose I buy a pair of electric hedge cutters from a local store, and suffer an electric shock while using them in the proper fashion. Under the Sale of Goods Act (Chapter Two) the seller has a duty to ensure that the cutters are reasonably fit for their purpose, which they are proved not be be by the fact that this accident happened. He is accordingly liable. But if it is not I who am injured but my wife, to whom I have just given the cutters, the case becomes infinitely more complicated. She has no contractual relationship with the seller since she did not buy the goods, and so must prove negligence against someone. On the face of it that someone is unlikely to be the seller, since he will have no reason to suspect there is anything wrong with the goods or to test or dismantle every pair just in case, and it is therefore probably the manufacturer. Because she is not the buyer, in other words, she has to sue the manufacturer instead of the retailer, and she also has a completely different burden of proof. But how can she prove that the manufacturer—or, who knows, perhaps a sub-contractor, or an importer or distributor—was negligent? We must say again that the mere fact of an accident does not prove negligence. A surgeon may take all possible care in an operation but he cannot guarantee success. Drug manufacturers may subject their products to every conceivable test. If tragic side effects then appear, they will not be liable. They have done their best, and that is all the law of tort presently expects of them.

We have assumed thus far that manufacturers' liability must be non-contractual, but in fact this is not always so. We shall therefore consider briefly the rare cases where manufacturers might be *contractually* liable to injured users, and then examine in more detail what is meant by negligence.

Manufacturers' Guarantees
When we discussed the requirement of consideration in Chapter One we mentioned the difficulty it created in the way of enforcing manufacturers' promises, or guarantees as we shall call them here. Except where a manufacturer sells directly to the public the buyer plainly contracts with the *retailer*, and the consideration he gives him is payment or the promise of payment in return for the goods. That being so, when and how could he be said to contract with the manufacturer, *i.e.* to give consideration in return for the manufacturer's guarantee, without which the guarantee is not legally enforceable?

The answer is provided by the "collateral contract" idea, one contract alongside another, as illustrated in Chapter Two by the case of *Carlill* v. *Carbolic Smoke Ball Co*. In effect the manufacturers in that case said in their advertisement: "If you buy our goods from a retailer and use them in the appropriate fashion, we promise in return to prevent influenza and pay you if we fail." So in this and a handful of other cases the guarantees were enforced because they led buyers to make contracts with retailers; *Shanklin Pier* v. *Detel Products*, 1951; *Wells* v. *Buckland Sand*, 1964. In each of these, however, the buyer knew of the guarantee before he bought the goods, and so could fairly be said to be buying them partly in return for the guarantee. But what if he only came across the guarantee *after* he bought the goods? There may be ways round

·this difficulty. The buyer might argue that although he did not know for sure there was a guarantee or what its terms were, he bought on the assumption that the goods were guaranteed. Or he might give consideration subsequently, *e.g.* by putting a stamp on the guarantee card which he returns to the manufacturer, or by giving up certain legal rights he might have against the manufacturer in return for the manufacturer's promises. Neither of these arguments has been tested in the courts and the position remains doubtful.

There do not in fact seem to be many cases of manufacturers actually denying their obligations under guarantees, but there are certainly numerous complaints about the limitations or unfairness of such undertakings. According to a recent Office of Fair Trading report local authorities received over a thousand complaints about guarantees in a six month period. They concerned guarantees which were in the name of the buyer only and could not be transferred, or which were too short and had expired before the goods could be repaired, or were subject to strict conditions such as immediate return of the guarantee card. In Chapter Five we consider the new limitations upon the manufacturer's ability to opt out of liability by the terms of his guarantee.

Negligence

Failing any strict contractual liability to the users of his goods the manufacturer can only be liable—if at all—in negligence. Negligence can be very shortly defined as doing what a reasonable man would not do, or not doing what he would do. But what are the reasonable man's standards? There seem to be five main factors to be taken into account and balanced against each other in deciding what is reasonable; the likelihood of accident—on the common-sense basis that the more likely it is the more should be done to avoid it, and the less likely it is the less one could be expected to do anything at all about it: the seriousness of accident—again for the common sense reason that more precautions should be taken against grave (even though perhaps unlikely) risks than trivial ones: the obviousness of the risk: the cost of prevention—the vital economic factor—and lastly the inherent risks of the goods or services in question. The end result of balancing these factors one against the other is necessarily a compromise. One cannot tell in advance which factor the judge will find most important in any given case, and as we said earlier there is certainly no legal presumption that simply because an accident happens someone must be liable for it.

As a general rule the onus of proving negligence is upon the injured party, the plaintiff. We have hinted at the difficulties this may involve. The fault may actually be that of a component supplier, not the main manufacturer; *Taylor* v. *Rover Car Co.*, 1966. If the plaintiff does not know this and so sues the wrong party he may be liable for that party's costs—and he may also find himself barred by the passage of time from suing the right party. (Tort claims must be begun within three years of the accident or of the plaintiff knowing he has a right of action; contractual claims within six years of the breach of contract.) How then is the plaintiff supposed to know what went wrong in the production process, or whose fault it was? It is true he need not "lay his finger upon the exact person in all the chain who was responsible," *Grant* v. *Australian Knitting Mills*, 1936—but he must make out a prima facie case of negligence against the defendant. So when a windscreen shattered for no apparent reason a year after purchase the user lost his claim against the manufacturer because it could have broken through a fault in fitting, not production; *Evans* v. *Triplex*, 1936. Very occasionally the consumer will be helped by the *res ipsa loquitur* rule ("the thing speaks for itself"(—though if so why does it not speak in English?)) This is a rule of evidence under which the burden of *disproving* negligence falls immediately upon the defendant where the circumstances of the accident point overwhelmingly to his negligence, *e.g.* where a hot water bottle developed a leak very soon after purchase and scalded the user. But no one suggested that the *res ipsa* rule should apply in *Donoghue* v. *Stevenson*, above, nor for example in the Thalidomide claims.

Another very important point to bear in mind is that usually English law will only allow a claim in negligence if the plaintiff has suffered physical injury or damage to his property. Pure economic loss—*i.e.* not arising from physical injury or damage—is not yet compensatable in non-contractual claims, except where it is caused by negligent advice; *S.C.M.* v. *Whittall*, 1971: *Hedley Byrne* v. *Heller*, 1964. Thus if goods are needed for business purposes but cannot be used because of defects caused by careless manufacture the would-be user cannot sue the manufacturer in negligence to recover his loss of profit (though if he were the buyer he could sue the seller if and insofar as the goods were not reasonably fit for their purpose; Chapter Two).

With these reservations let us consider a further half dozen or so cases which illustrate how the principles of negligence are applied. We might begin by observing not only that many raw materials are inherently dangerous but that no matter how carefully or safely goods are designed or manufactured they likewise must carry some risk of injury—if not from proper use then from carelessness, as, *e.g.* with scissors or hammers or nails or pins, or from exceptional susceptibility; *Board* v. *Hedley*, 1951—dermatitis from using detergent—or simply from wear and tear. *Pearson* v. *N.W. Gas Board*, 1968, is an instructive case on raw materials. A gas main, buried at the standard depth and so far as was known in good condition, was fractured by an exceptionally severe frost. The result was an explosion in which a house was destroyed, the husband killed and his wife severely injured. She claimed compensation for her losses from the Board, alleging negligence. The court held that on the evidence the Board had taken all the normally effective precautions and so could not be liable for failing to predict or prevent this tragic accident. The cost element is also clearly relevant. If the Board had been held liable in this quite exceptional case it would follow that it would have to spend limitless sums of money re-burying all its mains all over the country at a suitably greater depth—though even then no-one could say how much deeper they would have to be to ensure such an accident could never happen again. Only very occasionally has the use of a raw material actually been banned, but it might be so on grounds of likely or serious injury.

Often enough the inherent dangers to which we have referred can only be reduced by warnings as to the use of the materials or goods. Questions may then arise as to whether the warning was clear and adequate, or given to the right person. In *Allard* v. *Monahan*, 1974 (Can.), an experienced contractor was killed by the ricochet of a nail he had fired from a nail gun. His widow sued the manufacturer of the gun. The judge said: "It is true that a person . . . who deals in firearms must exercise a high standard of care in the conduct of his business, but that does not mean to say that he is obliged to supply or recommend every safety device which is on the market or can be made available. The manual which is supplied with this tool describes these devices and a person renting the tool can avail himself of this additional protection if he so desires." Since the contractor had not followed the advice in the manual the claim was lost. The manufacturer of hair dye in *Holmes* v. *Ashford*, 1950, knew that his product could be dangerous to certain skins. The hairdressers to whom the dye was supplied were notified of the dangers by a warning on the container. An injured client's claim that she also should have been warned was rejected. But where a product is designed for general use the warning must of course be clear and adequate for all members of the public; *Lambert* v. *Lastoplex Chemicals*, 1972 (Can.)—insufficient warning of highly inflammable material.

Are precautions still necessary if the danger is obvious? In *Crow* v. *Barford*, 1963, the manufacturer produced a motor mower which had a large grass ejection aperture. The user put his foot into the hole, and injured himself on the blade. He lost his claim against the manufacturers because of what was held to be an obvious hazard. But surely the question ought to be "Was the danger *necessary*?" not "Was it visible?" Any other answer simply encourages shoddy design. This case is also worth noting because it indicates the kind of defences manufacturers may have against consumers' claims—*e.g.* that the consumer has handled the goods wrongly, or agreed to run the risks involved. Even so, some forms of misuse are both predictable and preventable by the manufacturer. In *Spruill* v. *Boyle-Midway*, 1962 (United States), a young child ate some poisonous floor polish. It was held that since the company knew their product was poisonous and knew it was intended for household use—and on the floor—they should have anticipated some such mishap and put a warning on the tin. True the child might not have been able to read it but the parents could, and should safeguard it accordingly.

Negligence of Sellers and Distributors
This chapter has concentrated upon manufacturers' negligence but exactly the same problems of non-contractual liability may affect sellers and distributors, as in the following circumstances. In *Fisher* v. *Harrods*, 1966, a person bought a bottle of jewellery cleaner from Harrods which he sent to Mrs. Fisher. When she came to use it the bottle "exploded" and the liquid went into her eyes, causing pain and temporary blindness. The explosion

occurred because of the build up of pressure of the contents and the way the bottle was sealed. There was no warning of danger on the bottle. From what we have said above it might be thought that if anyone should be liable for the contents and sealing of the bottle, and for the absence of any warning, it must be the manufacturer. But in this particular case the manufacturer was a "man of straw"—someone not worth suing because he had no money. Mrs. Fisher therefore had no choice but to sue Harrods if she was to sue anyone at all. But while Harrods were the sellers Mrs. Fisher was not the buyer, and so she had to prove that Harrods were negligent and not merely that the bottle or contents were not reasonably fit for their purpose.

Harrods had tested the product originally to see whether it did what it was supposed to do, *i.e.* clean jewellery, and on being satisfied of this they sold it. Evidence was given by Harrods and a buyer from another leading store that it was not their practice to do anything more than test the efficiency of goods they sold—which the judge accepted as normally quite sufficient. To prove negligence Mrs. Fisher therefore had to show there was something abnormal about this particular article which demanded exceptional precautions by the retailer—inquiries about the safety of the goods or their containers, or the qualifications of the manufacturer. She succeeded because Harrods knew or ought to have known that a solvent strong enough to clean jewellery was inherently dangerous. This should have put them on their guard to inquire about the manufacturer's qualifications—which were in fact virtually non-existent—and the safe packaging of his goods. The same conclusion would no doubt be reached with regard to electrical and similar equipment with a range of hazards known to experts but hidden from consumers; *Goodchild* v. *Vaclight*, 1965—distributors liable for electrical faults in imported goods. Conversely if there were no reason to suspect any danger there would be no duty to make inquiries and so no liability for accidents which could have been avoided by making them.

Lastly we should note the case of *Devillez* v. *Boots*, 1962. Mr. Devillez bought a bottle of corn solvent from the defendants. After a bath he applied the solvent on his corn. As he was putting the bottle away it tipped over, the cork came out and the contents spilled over his private parts. He wiped himself and looked at the label on the bottle to see what else he should do, but no warning or advice was given. Later he suffered extreme pain and had to undergo plastic surgery. He sued Boots in all their capacities—as sellers, distributors and manufacturers of the product. We have no information about his claim in contract, but he might well have lost under that heading because the corn solvent was undoubtedly reasonably fit for its purpose, whatever harm it might do elsewhere. In alleging negligence Mr. Devillez was also in difficulty because Boots established that over the previous 30 years they had sold some 20 million bottles of this preparation under the same label and in the same type of bottle. During that time they had had only a dozen minor complaints. The judge accepted that such a successful and safe commercial record was very much in Boots' favour. He nonetheless held them liable for essentially the same reason we saw in *Fisher*, that they knew the preparation had quite a strong concentration of acid in it and so should have anticipated danger to other more tender parts of the body by providing a safer bottle and/or clearer warning.

We might conclude therefore that a plaintiff suing for breach of contract has usually a comparatively straightforward claim to bring against a readily available and responsive defendant, whereas a plaintiff suing in negligence may consider himself lucky if he can find the right party and overcome the much more difficult burden of proof. The distinction between the two types of case is fundamental to English law, but could fairly be said to be completely arbitrary in its effects. Reforms on product liability are proposed to remedy the capricious and unfair operation of this branch of the law.

Product Liability
The basic principle of what has come to be called product liability law has been accepted in America for the last twenty years or more, and is now the subject of a European agreement—the Strasbourg Convention of 1977—which Britain has signed but not yet acted upon. In a nutshell the principle imposes upon manufacturers of goods the same liability for physical injuries that a seller has to his buyer. To put it another way, the familiar strict liability of seller to buyer under a contract of sale is to be imposed in the non-contractual relationship of manufacturer and ultimate user. Negligence therefore ceases to be an issue, and all

the injured user will have to prove is that the goods which injured him were not reasonably fit for their purpose. This does *not* lead to the conclusion (as is often asserted) that manufacturers are going to be liable for all conceivable or inconceivable accidents, any more than sellers are liable for all misfortunes suffered by buyers—as we saw for example in *Spencer*, *Bartlett*, *Griffiths* and *Heil* in Chapter Two. The Pearson Report on compensation for personal injuries, 1978, supported the introduction of product liability in Britain, as did the English and Scottish Law Commissions in 1977. The Report said that in practice there would probably be only a marginal increase in the present small number of claims against manufacturers, which could be covered by insurance. The great attraction of the proposals is of course the simplification and rationalisation of the law—a point admirably expressed by an American court some years ago: "The purpose of such a holding is to see to it that the costs of injuries resulting from defective products are borne by the manufacturers that put such products on the market rather than by the injured persons who are powerless to protect themselves." A perhaps still more agreeable solution is that adopted recently in New Zealand. All claims for damages for personal injuries have been abolished and replaced by a rational and comprehensive insurance system. Unfortunately this was rejected by the Pearson Report.

CHAPTER FIVE

EXCLUSION CLAUSES AND OTHER UNFAIR TERMS

We have looked at length at the civil liabilities of suppliers of goods and services. The vital question here is how far a supplier can legally avoid or limit these liabilities. Until very recently one could say that businessmen could almost "get away with murder" in this respect, but the position has now changed dramatically in favour of the consumer. This is a classic example of the kind of contract clause once in common use:

"Normandy Ferries shall not be liable for the death of or any injury, damage, or loss, delay or accident to passengers, their apparel or baggage, whensoever, wheresoever and howsoever caused and whether by negligence of their servants or agents or by unseaworthiness of the vessel (whether existing at the time of embarkation or sailing or at any other time) or otherwise. Normandy Ferries may in its absolute discretion and without any liability whatsoever alter the ports of embarkation or disembarkation and time of sailing and arrival, change the route, call at any port whatsoever without previous notice to the passengers. A passenger accepts that Normandy Ferries give no condition or warranty express or implied that the vessel used for the carriage is fit for the carriage of passengers their baggage or accompanied vehicles.''

As time went on the abuses inherent in such total rejection of liability became more and more apparent, and within the self-imposed limits of so-called freedom of contract principles the judges made various attempts to control their worst effects. Some of the judges' decisions remain important, for instance those requiring that consumers be aware of the existence of exclusion clauses before any question of their being bound by them could arise, but overall they are as we shall see later in this chapter of limited scope and effect. The demand for more systematic and comprehensive protection led to increasing intervention by Parliament. The first major reform was the Supply of Goods (Implied Terms) Act, 1973, which effectively repealed section 55 of the Sale of Goods Act—a section which expressly allowed sellers to get out of the duties imposed by the Act. That reform was in turn re-enacted as part of a still more important and far-reaching statute, the Unfair Contract Terms Act, 1977.

The Unfair Contract Terms Act

The Scope of the Act
We shall examine the new Act section by section, in which the "grid" below may be helpful, and then look at the common law rules—those made by the judges—to see what significance they still have. To begin with, however, the scope of the Act should be noted. It does not deal with *all* unfair contract terms, but only with certain specified types. And despite its title the Act also regulates some of these provisions even when they are not used in contracts but appear for example in public notices or announcements; section 14.

The main effects of the
UNFAIR CONTRACT TERMS ACT 1977
on terms in contracts or notices (s.14) excluding or (s.13)
restricting liability for breach of contract and/or negligence

PARTY imposing term	Term imposed by CONTRACT made after 1.2.78		Term imposed by NOTICE to avoid liability otherwise arising after 1.2.78 (s.11)	
	VOID	VALID IF REASONABLE at the time the contract was made	VOID	VALID IF REASONABLE at the time liability would otherwise have arisen (s.11)
Generally—anyone doing so in the way of business (ss.1 and 14) including business occupiers (s.2) and suppliers of services in U.K. (s.3) or abroad (s.26), and the following parties in particular—subject to Exceptions below	excluding liability for death or injury caused by negligence (s.2) certain choices of law clauses (s.27)	excluding liability for other loss or damage caused by negligence (s.2) excluding liability for breach of contract with consumer or on standard form (ss.3 and 11) excluding liability for misrepresentation (s.8) requiring consumer to indemnify (s.4)	excluding liability for death or injury caused by negligence (s.2)	excluding liability for other loss or damage caused by negligence (s.2)
manufacturers' and other third parties' guarantees of consumer goods (s.5)	excluding liability for loss or damage caused by negligence (s.2)		excluding liability for loss or damage caused by negligence (s.2)	
sellers of goods, and creditors where the goods are obtained by H.P., including non-commercial transactions (s.6)	excluding liability for defective title excluding liability for unfitness of goods in consumer transaction (s.12)	excluding liability for unfitness of goods in non-consumer transactions (s12 and Sched.2)		
other suppliers of goods (e.g. in contracts for services or hire) (s.7)	excluding liability for unfitness of goods in consumer transactions (s.12)	excluding liability for defective title excluding liability for unfitness of goods in non-consumer transactions (s.12 and Sched.2)		

Exceptions (Sched.1 and s.29): insurers; persons creating, transferring or ending interests in land or patent, etc., rights: persons contracting on formation or dissolution of companies or on the rights or duties of companies or their members: persons contracting on terms required by law or incorporated or approved by a "competent authority" which is not itself a party to contract; carriage of goods by sea, except in favour of consumer

Exclusion clauses in contracts made by these parties are subject only to the rules of common law, which apply also to all the contracts and notices above

Excluding Liability for Negligence

The Act is almost entirely concerned to restrict the rights of *businesses* to exclude certain areas of liability, particularly liability for negligence. Businesses are not defined in detail, but section 14 indicates the necessary element of continuity of dealing by stating that they include professions and the activities of government departments and local and public authorities. Negligence is defined in section 1. It can be either the breach of an express or implied duty in a contract to take reasonable care, or breach of the common law duty of care which arises independently of contract (as explained and illustrated in Chapter Four), or of the duty of an occupier under the Occupiers' Liability Act, 1957, to take reasonable care for the safety of his visitors. It does not matter whether such breach of duty is deliberate or inadvertent, nor whether the fault is personal or vicarious (*i.e.* imposed because of the wrongful act of an employee or other person for whom the business may be responsible).

Section 2 (1) says that any attempt by a business to exclude liability for death or injury caused by negligence is of no effect, whether the purported exclusion is by contract or notice. It may be difficult to decide whether functions such as charity meetings are "businesses" or not; *White* v. *Blackmore*, 1972. Although section 2 (1) makes such exclusions of liability null and void, it does actually forbid the use of these clauses in contracts or notices. An unscrupulous dealer or occupier might continue to use them and hope to convince an injured party thereby that he has no rights worth pursuing. The Office of Fair Trading has recognised this possibility and will recommend prohibition if need be, as it did in the Consumer Transactions (Restrictions on Statements) Order, below. We should emphasise also that the rule only applies to death or injury caused by negligence. Death or injury might be caused by circumstances over which a business occupier has little or no control, say the inherently dangerous nature of his products or operations. In that case the effect of section 2 (1) is certainly not to annul any warning notice he might put up, nor even to discourage him from putting one up. On the contrary, it would be negligent *not* to put up a notice, if and insofar as that was the only effective way, or one of the only effective ways, of reducing the danger.

Section 2 (2) permits businesses to exclude liability for *other* forms of loss or damage (*e.g.* damage to property) if it is fair and reasonable to do so. The reasonableness of a contract term excluding such liability is decided by reference to the parties' knowledge of the circumstances at the time the contract was made, but if a notice is used we have to look at the position when the liability arose or but for the notice would have arisen. No more specific guidance is given as to when a clause might or might not be fair or reasonable, but when the courts have to look at exclusion clauses in cloakrooms or in employers' or bankers' references and the like they will probably consider much the same factors as those listed below in connection with sections 6 and 7—exclusion of liability in certain sale, hire-purchase and ser e transactions.

Not all forms of loss or damage to property are caused by negligence. As we noted in Chapter Three, when a person pays to park his car he usually pays only for the space and does not thereby make the car park owner responsible for the vehicle's safety. The question of the car park owner's negligence if the car were stolen or damaged could not then arise.

Excluding Liability for Breach of Contract
The next rule, section 3, gives substantial protection against abuse of bargaining power not only to consumers as against retailers but also to retailers or other small businessmen contracting with more powerful businesses. A person "deals as a consumer" if he makes a contract which is not in the course of his own business, nor at an auction, nor by tender, but which is in the course of the other party's business, and any goods involved are of a kind ordinarily bought for private use or consumption; section 14. Retailers and other businessmen are within the section if they contract on another business's written standard terms. The section says that contract terms imposed on consumers or smaller businesses which purport to limit or exclude liability for the stronger party's breach of contract, or which seem to enable him to carry out his contract in a different way, or not perform it at all, are enforceable only if they are reasonable in the circumstances. The possible injustice of holding a retailer strictly liable, which we noted in Chapter Two, is thus very much reduced by ensuring that any claims he in turn might have against his supplier will not be defeated by an unfair exclusion clause.

Many familiar types of exclusion clause are regulated by this section, for example those used by laundries and travel agencies. Not all are necessarily unreasonable. It might be quite fair for an agency to protect itself against the consequences of bad weather or strike action, and the traveller in turn may protect himself by insurance. Section 11 tells us that where someone seeks to limit his liability under a contract to a certain sum of money, special attention must be paid to his resources and whether he could reasonably be expected to insure himself against such claims; *Levison* v. *Patent Steam Carpet Cleaning*, 1977.

Indemnity Clauses
Terms in contracts requiring consumers to indemnify some other person against liability incurred by that other for breach of contract or negligence are unenforceable unless reasonable in the circumstances; section 4. Such clauses may be found for example in car servicing contracts where dealers claim the right to move customers' cars without incurring liability for damage thereby caused to other vehicles. It is doubtful whether a clause of this kind could now be regarded as reasonable in this context.

Manufacturers' Guarantees
In Chapter Four we noted certain legal problems in enforcing manufacturers' guarantees. The object of section 5 is to ensure that any legal effect guarantees may have shall be beneficial—in general only conferring rights, not taking them away. The section applies to consumer goods in consumer use, *i.e.* not used exclusively for business purposes. Guarantee terms or notices relating to such goods are of no effect insofar as they exclude or restrict liability for loss or damage caused by the manufacturer's or supplier's negligence. Anything in writing is a guarantee if it contains a promise or assurance that defects will be made good. Manufacturers are already prevented from excluding liability for death or injury by section 2, above. But section 5 (3) states that this additional protection does *not* apply to the actual buyer or hire-purchaser of the goods. This may seem to nullify the whole section, but in fact simply establishes that its concern is with the ultimate user only. Buyers and hire-purchasers as such do not need the protection of section 5 because of the alternative rights they already have against sellers and owners, which are confirmed by section 6.

Exclusion of Buyers' and Hire-Purchasers' Rights

Section 6 is of fundamental importance for consumers, although strictly it does no more than re-enact rules introduced by the Supply of Goods (Implied Terms) Act, 1973. Effectively the section brings to an end the previously almost unchallenged rights of sellers and owners to opt out of the various implied duties we described in Chapter Two. It declares first that no seller or owner can escape liability for failing to give good title to buyers or hire-purchasers; p. 16. So far as the vital duties to supply goods corresponding with their description and/or sample, of merchantable quality and resonably fit for their purpose (pp. 18, 23) are concerned the section distinguishes between consumer transactions and non-consumer transactions. We have already seen how the Act defines "dealing as a consumer." In such transactions the business seller or owner *cannot in any circumstances* avoid liability for breach of any of these three conditions. Not only are exclusion clauses relating to these conditions void but any statement or notice to the contrary (*e.g.* "No refunds") is a criminal offence under the Consumer Transactions (Restrictions on Statements) Order, 1978.

In non-consumer transactions, *i.e.* contracts between businesses, liability for description, sample, merchantability and reasonable fitness can be excluded, but only if the exclusion clause satisfies the test of reasonableness. We mentioned earlier the protection given to the small businessman who has to deal on another's written standard forms; section 3. We see in the present section another version of the same rule—businesses are free to limit their liabilities between themselves, if and in so far as the limitation in question is reasonable.

Section 7 makes much the same provision as section 6 as to the fitness of goods which are not sold or hire-purchased but hired or provided under contracts for services, *e.g.* repair. The only difference between the two sections is that under section 7 suppliers can avoid liability for defective title, again subject to the test of reasonableness.

But what is "reasonable"? We have used the word over and over again but so far with only one or two general indications of what it might involve. Schedule 2 of the Act gives more specific guidance as to its meaning in the context of sections 6 and 7. The Schedule requires the court to consider in particular the relative bargaining power of the parties; whether other sources of supply are available; whether the customer received any inducement to agree to the terms, such as a lower price in return for a greater risk; whether other suppliers offered similar contracts without excluding liability; whether the customer knew of the existence and/or extent of the exclusion; whether any pre-condition of liability could practically be complied with, *e.g.* notification within seven days, and whether the goods were made to the customer's own specifications. The burden of proving that a term is reasonable is upon the party putting it forward—the seller or supplier.

Misrepresentation

Section 8 of the Unfair Contract Terms Act restates a rule introduced by the Misrepresentation Act, 1967—that a term in a contract excluding or restricting liability for pre-contractual statements will only be upheld subject to the same requirement of reasonableness. As we noted in Chapter One such clauses are frequently used in standard form contracts to exclude liability for statements in advertisements and sales literature. Whether the buyer has any remedy when goods or services supplied differ from those advertised will depend no doubt on his familiarity with standard forms and the extent to which he understood or could have understood the significance of the exclusion clause—which will depend in turn not only on what it says but on where and how the clause appears, size of print and factors of that kind. The same considerations apply to the representation itself. In *Cremdean Properties* v. *Nash*, 1977, for instance, a buyer was held entitled to allege misrepresentation as to the size of the property despite a clause that "accuracy is not guaranteed and the purchaser must satisfy himself" as to the particulars.

In section 9 the Act declares that if a contract term is subject to the test of reasonableness it remains so whether or not the contract as a whole has been broken or repudiated; *Harbutt's Plasticine* v. *Wayne Tank*, below. Section 10 prevents evasion of liability by means of a related or secondary contract. We should take account also of sections 13 and 27. Section 13 explains that terms declared void by the Act include those which admit liability but only on onerous or restrictive conditions, or which restrict any right or remedy or penalise a person seeking to enforce his rights. Clauses limiting the amount of compensation, charging for repairs, requiring complaints to be made within a very short time of delivery, or making the supplier's decision final, would come within this rule, but written agreements to submit to independent arbitration are valid. Section 27 states that the Act does not apply where parties who would not otherwise be bound by English law have voluntarily made it the law governing their contract, but that the Act is effective where another country's law has been adopted simply in order to evade it.

These are the main provisions of the Act, repeated in sections 15–25 in terms appropriate to the law of Scotland. It has as we have seen a very extensive coverage and must be of the greatest benefit to the consumer and in some respects to small businesses. But we should also note its limitations. Certain non-consumer transactions are either not provided for or are less well regulated than consumer contracts. Liability for defective services (as distinct from goods provided in the course of those services) can still sometimes be excluded. Section 29 says that the Act does not affect terms required or approved by statute or treaty. A term approved by a "competent authority"—a court, arbitrator, government department or public authority—is presumed to satisfy the test of reasonableness. Codes of practice approved by the Office of Fair Trading, p. 77, might therefore give certain trades or industries an appropriate degree of immunity which would otherwise be forbidden. Several more specific exceptions are made in Schedule 1. These are listed on the "grid" on p. 51 and need not be repeated here.

Apart from the new Act are several other statutes regulating the use of exclusion clauses in various more limited circumstances. So for example the Consumer Credit Act invalidates any term in a consumer credit or hire agreement inconsistent with the protection given to debtors or hirers by the Act. The Defective Premises Act, 1972, imposes duties of good workmanship upon builders which cannot be excluded. Another Act forbids solicitors to exclude liability for negligence. Hotel proprietors are liable within certain limits for any property of overnight guests which is lost, stolen or damaged, whether or not through the negligence of the hotel staff. A group of Acts regulate the terms of domestic and international transport of people and goods. The Road Traffic Act, for instance, declares void any contract terms which purport to restrict liability for the death or injury of passengers in public service vehicles.

The Common Law

Although suppliers' freedom to dictate their own terms is very much reduced by the Unfair Contract Terms Act and other measures listed above the rules made by our judges about exclusion clauses still have a significant part to play. They may affect consumers' rights both in circumstances not yet regulated by statute and even where there is statutory provision. As we shall see their main effect is to determine whether such a clause is part of the contract in the first place. If not, no question of its reasonableness or otherwise under the Unfair Contract Terms Act could arise. And even where accepted as part of the contract the clause may be invalidated because the supplier's breach of contract goes so far beyond its terms that again its reasonableness is not relevant. It should be understood, however, that the rules we are about to consider are not so much rules of law as merely principles of construction or interpretation which the judges would apply to any other kind of disputed wording in a contract.

The first rule or principle is one of reasonable notice. An exclusion clause could not be effective unless the consumer knew of its existence. The supplier need not ensure that the consumer reads or understands the clause but only that he has a fair opportunity to do so. This may require no more than a phrase such as "For conditions see over," but more recent decisions suggest that the clause must not simply be available but clearly an exclusion of liability; *Thompson* v. *L.M.S. Ry.*, 1930: *Mendelssohn* v. *Normand*, 1969. Secondly the document or notice containing the exclusion clause must appear as part of the contract and not just as a receipt or note which the consumer might properly disregard; *Chapelton* v. *Barry U.D.C.*, 1940—deckchair ticket had no contractual effect: *Parker* v. *S.E. Ry.*, 1877—terms on left luggage ticket binding because depositor knew he could only get his luggage back in accordance with them. Similarly the exclusion clause must not be added in after the contract has been made; *Thornton* v. *Shoe Lane Parking*, 1971—notice inside car park ineffective: *Olley* v. *Marlborough Court*, 1949—notice limiting hotel's liability should have been at reception desk and not in hotel bedroom. Difficulties might arise in deciding exactly when the contract was made, as we said in Chapter One. Both parties may contract on the understanding that detailed particulars will be provided at a later date, which could then still be regarded as part of the contract; *British Crane Hire* v. *Ipswich Plant Hire*, 1976. But probably only businessmen accustomed to dealing in this way would be bound by such terms; *Hollingworth* v. *Southern Ferries*, 1977. Alternatively a customer might be bound by terms he had become aware of through previous dealings with the supplier; *McCutcheon* v. *McBrayne*, 1964. Another rule is that an exclusion clause is invalid if the supplier misrepresents or varies its effect, whether orally or in writing; *Curtis* v. *Chemical Cleaning*, 1951: *Evans* v. *Merzario*, 1976.

Next is the rule that ambiguous or obscure clauses will be interpreted in the way least favourable to the party relying on them—the supplier; *Ashington Piggeries* v. *Hill*, 1971. In particular it will be presumed that the exclusion refers only to contractual liability and not to liability for negligence unless the wording clearly covers negligence or could have no other application. Conversely if a clause is clear and unambiguous the consumer who signs the contract containing it is bound by it, subject perhaps to the rule about notice, above, and the doctrine of fundamental breach discussed below; *L'Estrange* v. *Graucob*, 1934. Exclusion clauses normally protect only the person putting them forward, but if an employer expressly contracts on behalf of his employees or agents they also may escape liability; *Adler* v. *Dickson*, 1955: *N.Z. Shipping* v. *Satterthwaite*, 1974.

Lastly we come to what is probably the judges' most determined attempt to control exclusion clauses, the doctrine of fundamental breach. This is the principle or presumption that contracting parties do not wish to make ineffective or meaningless contracts and that clauses which would have that effect by denying liability for any and every breach should therefore be disregarded; *Suisse Atlantique* v. *N.V. Rotterdamsche Kolen Centrale*, 1967. The basic difficulty is of course in deciding how serious a breach has to be to go "beyond the limit"—which may be the difference between supplying completely useless goods and those which are "merely" very faulty, a fine and eventually untenable distinction; *Karsales* v. *Wallis*, 1956: *Handley* v. *Marston*, 1962. Another problem is that what may look like an exclusion clause is just a limited commitment by the supplier. If he promises very little to begin with he cannot be criticised for not providing more. The doctrine has, however, enabled the courts to say that liability for fraudulent or criminal conduct cannot be excluded. This would include, *e.g.* a false statement that goods have been examined before purchase or bought without reliance on the seller's skill and judgment; *Lowe* v. *Lombank*, 1960. There is no definite rule that liability for deliberate breach of contract cannot be excluded, since the consequences of the breach might still be trivial, or the breach justified by an emergency.

It follows from the *Suisse Atlantique* decision, above, that while contracting parties might be *unlikely* to agree on terms nullifying the main objects of their contracts, they could nevertheless expressly commit themselves to such wording, in which case their wishes would have to be upheld. In later cases the courts have tried to avoid this conclusion. Perhaps the most vexed of recent decisions is *Harbutt's Plasticine* v. *Wayne Tank*, 1970, where goods and services were supplied as per contract but being of defective design caused a fire which burned the premises to the ground. The supplier's liability was limited under the contract to a small sum, but he was still held liable for the full amount. The argument was that since the subject matter of the contract had been destroyed the consumer was not bound by the contract or the exclusion clause it contained. This decision raised further difficulties, as to the effect for example of *partial* destruction or of a clause denying the consumer's right to repudiate, which were duly resolved by section 9 of the Unfair Contract Terms Act, above.

One more matter remains for discussion in this chapter—the extent to which the law regulates unfair terms generally, as distinct from exclusion clauses in particular. In the past the law has almost always left the parties to decide for themselves whether their bargain is a fair one, but in very recent years it has shown a greater willingness to intervene over this question. An important statutory example is section 139 of the Consumer Credit Act, which enables the court to set aside "extortionate" credit transactions. The common law is also shifting its position, slightly but perceptibly. We could not say there is yet any general prohibition of "unconscionable dealing" such as may be found in other European systems and the American Uniform Commercial

Code, but in two or three cases abuse of bargaining power has been found and condemned in terms which are undoubtedly novel in English law.

Perhaps the most interesting example of what might with some hesitation be called the new trend is *Lloyds Bank* v. *Bundy*, 1974. An old man anxious to support his son's business mortgaged all his own land to the bank in return for a loan to his son. When the business failed the bank foreclosed. The Court of Appeal held the transaction unenforceable because there was a relationship of trust between the bank and the old man under which the bank should have ensured that he had independent advice before risking the loss of all his assets. Lord Denning reached this conclusion by drawing together various strands of the common law; long standing rules protecting weaker parties against, for example, "undue influence"—by a parent over a child, or a doctor over a patient—or abuse of an official position to "gain more than is justly due," and the like. He went on: "Gathering all together, I would suggest that through all these instances there runs a single thread. They rest on 'inequality of bargaining power.' By virtue of it, the English law gives relief to one who, without independent advice, enters into a contract on terms which are very unfair or transfers property for a consideration which is grossly inadequate, when his bargaining power is grievously impaired by reason of his own needs, or desires, or by his own ignorance or infirmity, coupled with undue influences or pressures brought to bear on him by or for the benefit of the other. When I use the word 'undue' I do not mean to suggest that the principle depends on proof of any wrongdoing. The one who stipulates for an unfair advantage may be moved solely by his own self-interest, unconscious of the distress he is bringing to the other. I have also avoided any reference to the will of the one being 'dominated' or 'overcome' by the other. One who is in extreme need may knowingly consent to a most improvident bargain, solely to relieve the straights in which he finds himself. Again, I do not mean to suggest that every transaction is saved by independent advice. But the absence of it may be fatal. With these explanations, I hope this principle will be found to reconcile the cases."

Similarly in *Schroeder* v. *Macauley*, 1974, the House of Lords recognised the principle of "protection of those whose bargaining power is weak against being forced by those whose bargaining power is stronger to enter into bargains that are unconscionable." And in *Davis* v. *W.E.A. Records*, 1975, Lord Denning condemned the behaviour of the manager of a "pop group" who had taken the copyright of the group's music (for want of a better word!) for a consideration of one shilling for each work and who undertook no obligations in return. He said it was unconscionable also that the group should have agreed to such terms from a position of economic dependence and without the advice of a lawyer.

From these various remarks we can see interesting possibilities of development in the law, enabling our judges if they so decide to intervene on the consumer's behalf in ways as yet uncontemplated by Act of Parliament.

CHAPTER SIX

ILLEGAL ADVERTISING AND HIGH PRESSURE SALES TECHNIQUES— COMPLAINTS AND CONTROLS

Illegal Advertising

So far we have discussed what the consumer can do—or must do—for him or herself if he or she has suffered loss or injury through faulty goods or unsatisfactory service and the supplier or manufacturer will not make amends. Fortunately legal proceedings are not always necessary. The threat of such proceedings may encourage the other side to make an offer in settlement, and in any case most businesses nowadays realise that they only give themselves a bad name by being difficult over claims they really ought to meet. But problems of cheats and shoddy goods and accidents will no doubt be with us for ever, and it is not every consumer who either wants to or is able to threaten legal action—a possibly expensive and certainly nerve-racking and time-consuming prospect. Most of us would prefer someone else to fight our battles for us, or, better still, that we should have laws which make the problems less likely to arise in the first place.

These are in part the functions of the criminal law, by which most of the rules we turn to now are enforced.

The Trade Descriptions Act

The criminal law cannot stop a person making a bad bargain, nor can it prevent all inferior or faulty goods from coming onto the market. It is bound to be both limited and selective in its approach. Its original concern was with shopkeepers' weighing and measuring scales, and with the purity of food and drink. These often very technical and detailed rules are now in the Weights and Measures Acts, 1963–79, and the Food and Drugs Act, 1955, referred to again below, and in the countless regulations made under those Acts. The most immediately relevant measure, however, is the Trade Descriptions Act of 1968, as amended in 1972, which is aimed at the problem of deceptive advertising. The Office of Fair Trading, whose work is described at the end of this chapter, tells us there are some 600,000 consumer complaints a year. Only about 65,000 of these represent possible infringements of the criminal law, which for consumer protection purposes comprises 30 or so Acts and many subsidiary regulations, but more than half of the 65,000 are issues arising under the Trade Descriptions Act alone. These in turn lead to some 1,500 prosecutions every year. The Act is enforced by local authority Weights and Measures or Trading Standards Departments. The penalties for breaking it can be severe—an unlimited fine and/or up to two years' imprisonment.

Compensation Orders
From the consumer's point of view this is a very useful way of tackling this particular evil. If he thinks he has been deceived he will be much more willing to call in at the town hall to make a complaint, and leave the inspectors to pursue it, than he would be to embark on legal proceedings on his own account. The Act does not affect his civil rights, so that he could still sue for damages for fraud or misrepresentation if he wanted to. Equally it does not help him at all on the questions discussed in previous chapters, *i.e.* where goods or services prove defective or dangerous *without* any misleading advertising being involved. In these cases he must decide for himself whether he wishes to sue. But consumers

who are out of pocket because traders have committed offences under the Trade Descriptions Act or other such criminal legislation are greatly assisted by the Powers of Criminal Courts Act, 1973. This Act enables criminal courts to make compensation orders—in effect awards of damages—as part of the defendant's punishment. All the consumer need do then is give evidence of his loss in the course of the prosecution, though whether he will be fully compensated depends on any other penalty imposed and the defendant's ability to pay.

Goods

We shall consider in turn the main provisions of the Trade Descriptions Act on advertisements of goods, price reductions, and services, and then note the defences open to advertisers charged with breach of the Act. Section 1 makes it an offence to "apply a false trade description" to goods *in the course of a trade or business*. Mere "application" is sufficient; no question of the trader's good or bad faith arises at this stage. But at the same time he cannot be liable unless he knows that what he is saying or doing amounts to a statement of some sort about his goods. So in *Cottee* v. *Seaton*, 1972, no offence was committed by a dealer who sold a car quite unaware of repair work undertaken, and concealed, by a previous owner. A trade description may be "applied" by writing, word of mouth, or conduct. A car's odometer or mileometer, for example, makes a statement about its mileage which the seller appears to endorse. To avoid liability for a mileometer which for all he knows may be false the seller must use means which are at least as "bold, precise and compelling" as the original statement. He should therefore either cover the mileometer or give a very clear written warning at the time of sale and in the contract itself that he takes no responsibility for the alleged mileage, or preferably both; *R.* v. *Hammerton*, 1976. (In a survery conducted in 1978 by the Office of Fair Trading some 50 per cent. of used cars sold by dealers were found to have been the subject of odometer frauds. Increasingly heavy penalties are being imposed.) The false statement need not be made by the dealer in his capacity as seller; *Fletcher* v. *Budgen*, 1974—dealer liable for making untrue statement about car he was buying on "trade in" basis. Statements made by a dealer when providing a service, *e.g.* offering advice and not actually supplying goods, or made after a sale of goods has been completed are outside the Act; *Wickens* v. *Hall*, 1972.

Sections 2 and 3 are key sections explaining what a "trade description" is and when such a description is "false." Section 2 begins:

"(1) A trade description is an indication, direct or indirect, and by whatever means given, of any of the following matters with respect to any goods or parts of goods, that is to say—

(a) quantity, size or gauge;
(b) method of manufacture, production, processing or re-conditioning;
(c) composition;
(d) fitness for purpose, strength, performance, behaviour or accuracy;
(e) any physical characteristics not included in the preceding paragraphs;
(f) testing by any person and results thereof;
(g) approval by any person or conformity with a type approved by any person;
(h) place or date of manufacture, production, processing or reconditioning;
(i) person by whom manufactured, produced, processed or reconditioned;
(j) other history, including previous ownership or use."

The purpose of this list is to cover as many matters of *fact* as possible whose truth or falsity can be tested accordingly. The weakness of this approach is of course that loopholes appear. Since there is no precise reference to the *worth* or *value* of goods, for example, a trader is free to make as many vague or false statements about that aspect of his goods as he pleases. So "Worth double," "Best on the market," etc., are evidently to be regarded as expressions of opinion—trader's puff, which the consumer's own common sense should enable him to weigh and disregard; *Cadbury* v. *Halliday*, 1975—label claimed "Extra Value," though price, size and content exactly the same as before—no liability. But when in *Robertson* v. *Diciccio*, 1972, a salesman described a car as "beautiful" the court said this word referred not only to its appearance but to its "fitness" and "performance" (section 2 (1) (*d*)) and since it was in fact in poor working order he was found guilty. Beauty should evidently be more than skin deep! It is not clear who has to prove or disprove the truth of an advertisement, though one might think the onus should be upon the advertiser.

An advertiser cannot yet be required to publish corrections of false statements, though the Department of Prices and Consumer Protection announced proposals to that effect in 1978.

Under section 3 the test is whether the trade description is "false to a material degree," whether or not anyone was deceived thereby. Small discrepancies might sometimes be both unavoidable and unimportant. In *R* v. *Ford Motor Co.*, 1974, it was held that whether a car could properly be sold as "new" (section 2 (1) (*h*)) & (*j*)) following repairs by the dealer depended on the extent and nature of the damage, and the quality of the repairs. A trade description might also be false for legal purposes if simply "misleading" as to one of the matters specified in section 2, although not actually untrue. So a label on a bottle of whisky showing a Scottish scene or tartan pattern could still be illegal despite a small but correct declaration on the label that it was made in some other country. Similarly a statement which though not within section 2 could be taken as such will lead to liability if materially false.

The interesting and important problem of "slack fill" should be noted in this context. Many goods are supplied in containers whose size bears little or no relation to their contents, and which seem designed to deceive the consumer. Sometimes containers have to state the weight of their contents, but even so it could surely be argued that the size of a container is "an indication, direct or indirect and by whatever means given" as to the "quantity, size or gauge" of the goods inside, and if unnecessarily large must be "misleading". Strangely enough however there appears to be no agreed policy on this matter, and the writer has been referred to only one successful prosecution, reported in records which are not available to the general public.

Price Reductions

The next major issue in the Act is that of false statements of price; section 11. Only three forms of deception are provided for. First it is an offence for a supplier to suggest falsely that his price is equal to or less than a recommended price. This means a price recommended by the manufacturer or producer and applicable in the area where the goods are offered, unless the contrary is stated. Secondly, the supplier must not indicate that he is offering goods at a price lower than their actual price. To charge more than a stated price is prima facie an infringement of the section—*Whitehead* v. *Collett*, 1975—as is for example a label on goods proclaiming in large letters "5p off" and in tiny print "your next purchase." It must be clear whether the price includes V.A.T.; *Richards* v. *Westminster Motors*, 1975. Thirdly the seller must not falsely claim reductions in his own previous prices. But how can it be shown whether a purported reduction is genuine? The Act says that unless the price label states otherwise, the reduction is presumed to be from the price the seller has charged for those goods for at least 28 consecutive days in the preceding six months; section 11 (3) (*a*) (ii). The onus of proving the seller has not sold at that price for that length of time is upon the prosecution—a quite impossible task; *House of Holland* v. *Brent L.B.C.*, 1971.

Services

We turn now to advertisements for services. These are dealt with by section 14, which makes it an offence for anyone in the course of business knowingly or recklessly (*M.F.I. Warehouses* v. *Nattrass*, 1971) to make either a false statement about any of the following, or any statement likely to be taken as such (*British Airways* v. *Taylor*, 1975);

"(i) the provision in the course of any trade or business of any services, accommodation or facilities;
(ii) the nature of any services, accommodation or facilities provided in the course of any trade or business;
(iii) the time at which, manner in which or persons by whom any services, accommodation or facilities are so provided;
(iv) the examination, approval or evaluation by any person of any services, accommodation or facilities so provided; or
(v) the location or amenities of any accommodation so provided."

This section follows the pattern of listing offences rather than laying down one general offence—and so again there are loopholes. It is not certain for example whether the phrase "services, accommodation or facilities" applies to sales of land as such, in which case many of the optimistic statements in builders' and estate agents' advertisements may be beyond the reach of the Act; *Breed* v. *Cluett*, 1970. Various other statements may also slip through the net. To give an impression of reliability, for example, a trader might quite deliberately and falsely say that his firm had been in business for a hundred years—but that would not be a direct statement about the services he was offering and so would not be caught by the Act. Services provided under contracts of employment are specifically excluded.

Perhaps the most difficult question regarding services is that posed by cases such as *Beckett* v. *Cohen* and *R.* v. *Sunair Holidays*, both in 1973. In *Beckett* a builder promised to build a garage to a particular design and within an agreed time, knowing that he might be unable to finish the job and in the event failing to do so. On the face of it this was a promise within the terms of section 14 (i) and (iii), but the court said that the problem was essentially one of breach of contract and that great care had to be taken before making mere breaches of contract into crimes. Accordingly in this and the *Sunair* case, where various hotel amenities were promised but not provided, it was held that a promise of future services could only be criminal if it could be *proved untrue at the time it was made*—a considerable reduction in the apparent scope of the Act. A travel agency could therefore be criminally liable for booking rooms in a hotel which had not been built, for example, but not for promising services which could have been provided but were not. The agency might still of course be liable civilly; Chapter Three. A trader who tries to repudiate a promise, *e.g.* by denying his liability under a guarantee, might thereby indicate that the promise was false at the time he made it; *Bambury* v. *Hounslow L.B.C.*, 1971.

Defences

The last main area of interest in the Trade Descriptions Act is in section 24. This says that a person charged with breach of the rules discussed above can escape liability if he can prove:

"(1) (a) that the commission of the offence was due to a mistake or to reliance on information supplied to him or to the act or default of another person, an accident or some other cause beyond his control; and

(b) that he took all reasonable precautions and exercised all due diligence to avoid the commission of such an offence by himself or any person under his control" (or)

(3) ". . . that he did not know, and could not with reasonable diligence have ascertained, that the goods did not conform to the description or that the description had been applied to the goods."

Under paragraphs (a) and (b) the defendant must show that the wrong was someone else's fault and not his own fault. In *Tesco Supermarkets* v. *Nattrass*, 1972, the House of Lords held that "another person" could include the defendant's own employee, though the decision turned on the precautions which head office proved it had in fact taken and on the very substantial size of the organisation. In smaller enterprises where personal supervision is possible, the *Tesco* ruling should not provide any defence.

Section 24 (1) (*b*) above shows that it is not sufficient for the defendant just to accept another's word—he must make inquiries himself where practicable to test or confirm the truth of the matter. So where a trader advertised watches as "waterproof" in reliance on the manufacturer's erroneous assurance to that effect the court held that he could and should have tested one himself; *Sherratt* v. *Gerald*, 1970. Similarly a used-car dealer may need to contact the previous owner of a trade-in vehicle or have it examined by experts if the mileage is in doubt; *Naish* v. *Gore*, 1971. Decisions of this kind are undoubtedly very beneficial to the consumer.

Reforms
The Office of Fair Trading has suggested ways of making the Trade Descriptions Act more effective. It proposes for example that the items listed in section 2 should include the identity, standing or commercial importance of the supplier, the contents and authorship of books, records and the like, and the veracity of any alleged tests of the goods. (On the other hand, a proposed EEC Directive would simplify matters by a general prohibition of misleading advertising, which might be preferable.) As regards prices the OFT suggests that when "recommended prices" are quoted the manufacturer and retailer should be independent parties unless otherwise stated, and that claimed reductions should be tested by reference to prices charged over the previous 28 days. Another answer might be to compel the trader to state in writing what his own previous price was and how long it had been effective. The OFT has also said that the rules as to services should specifically include land, and that the difficulty posed by *Beckett* v. *Cohen*, above, should be resolved by making it illegal to promise services which the promisor has no intention or reasonable expectation of providing.

Certain changes were effected by the Price Marking (Bargain Offers) Order, 1979. With limited exceptions the Order forbids a retailer of consumer goods or services to claim reductions from his own previous prices (whether specified or not, *e.g.* "10p. off"), or reductions from someone else's prices for or valuation of the same goods or services (*e.g.* "Worth £100; our price £75"). But the Order does not apply if the retailer or another identified person has actually charged the higher price in the course of business, and reductions from manufacturers' recommended prices may also be claimed except in sales of beds.

Food and Drugs

There are of course many rules about the form and content of advertisements apart from those in the Trade Descriptions Act, all of them entitling consumers to complain to the appropriate authority and seek redress. We cannot examine all the rules here, but should mention their general scope and a few matters of particular interest. Most of the detailed regulations concern foodstuffs, and were made under the Foods and Drugs Act, 1955. The Act forbids advertising or sale of foodstuffs unfit for human consumption and advertising which misleads as to the nature, substance or quality of food and drugs. It is enforced by local authority environmental health inspectors. Labelling regulations require many foodstuffs to be labelled or advertised at the point of sale with their ingredients and the name and address of the packer or labeller. No general requirement has yet been introduced for the last date of sale or consumption to be marked. Health food claims are restricted by the Labelling of Food Regulations. Advertising of medicinal products is controlled by the Medicines Act, 1968. Public advertisements of cures for certain specified diseases are prohibited.

Difficult questions of degree may arise in enforcing food and drugs law, as was recognised by the House of Lords in the important case of *Smedley* v. *Breed*, 1974. Smedley's were prosecuted because of caterpillar larva found in a tin of peas despite the very elaborate precautions they had taken to exclude foreign matter. They had produced some 3,500,000 tins of peas that season and had had only four complaints. The court held that although strictly the company had to be found guilty, local authorities should keep a sense of proportion and consider whether prosecutions such as this were really necessary to protect the interests of consumers. Magistrates were advised that if they thought a prosecution unnecessary they might find liability but nonetheless grant an absolute discharge.

Weights and Measures

Similarly our weights and measures legislation, which plays a vital part in ensuring the truth of advertisements as to price and quantity of goods, has to allow for inevitable accident and "inconsiderable" deficiencies. A deficiency of up to perhaps three or four per cent. might be regarded as "inconsiderable" in a single article, but much depends on the type of article and average quantities in other such articles; *Cave* v. *Dudley Co-op.*, 1934.

Safety

More emphasis has been attached in recent years to the safety of other consumer goods besides food and drugs. Potentially the most important measure is the Consumer Safety Act, 1978—"potentially" because it is only an enabling Act; one which enables the Secretary of State to make rules about particular products, and it remains to be seen what use is made of it. His powers are to make *safety regulations* determining the construction, design, contents, packing, etc., of goods and the information to be given with them; to issue *prohibition orders* forbidding the sale of a particular type of article; to issue *prohibition notices* forbidding a particular trader to sell any specified article, and to serve *notices to warn* on individual traders requiring them to publish at their own expense warnings or advice about goods they have sold. The Act confers rights of consultation and appeal except in emergencies. Breach of these regulations or notices is a criminal offence, and anyone injured thereby may claim damages. Safety regulations made under the Consumer Protection Act, 1961, remain in force. Regulations affect oil heaters, nightdresses, carry cots, toys, electrical appliances, electric blankets, cooking utensils, domestic heating appliances, pencils, pens, crayons, etc., domestic electrical equipment, babies' dummies, prams, cosmetics and balloon making compounds.

Motor vehicles and accessories have been the subject of much highly specialised legislation. The principal Act is the Road Traffic Act, 1972, and the main regulations under it are the Motor Vehicles (Construction and Use) Regulations, 1974–78. These specify standards of vehicle design and equipment and the standards of fitness for numerous parts such as tyres, brakes, mirrors, speedometers, seat belts, etc. Sale or use of a vehicle in breach of these provisions is a criminal offence, but conviction does not of itself prove liability to anyone injured by the defective vehicle.

Price Displays

A number of very recent rules have gone a long way towards ensuring that the consumer knows exactly how much he has to pay for what he wants. The Price Marking (Food) Order, 1978, applies with certain exceptions to premises, including stalls and vehicles, where food and drink is offered for retail sale and requires that the price of the food or drink or a unit price be clearly shown. Food which the seller selects and hands or delivers to the consumer as directed by him is excluded, as is food consumed on the premises, and milk, bread and soft drinks delivered to the home. Another Order, made in 1979, requires that café and restaurant prices be clearly displayed outside the dining area. Orders have been made requiring the display of unit prices on meat—again with exceptions—and cheese. The repricing of food and drink items which have already been displayed at a marked price is forbidden by the Food (Prohibition of Repricing) Order, 1978. As regards accommodation, a 1977 Order requires premises with four or more bedrooms offering overnight accommodation to guests who have not booked in advance to display notices showing minimum and maximum overnight charges. Holiday camps and night sleeper trains are excluded. It is proposed also that prices of all goods and services should state specifically whether or not V.A.T. is included. Garages must show clearly and unambiguously the prices charged for the cheapest and dearest brands of petrol (and another display order which can conveniently be noted here is that requiring information on official fuel consumption figures to be shown on new cars offered for sale in showrooms and on forecourts. The figures must also be included in the car handbook and in any advertisements or sales literature referring to fuel consumption). Clear price marking is required in many of the codes of conduct drawn up by various trade associations in consultation with the Office of Fair Trading. Complaints that such codes have been broken should be made to the Trading Standards Department or the OFT or the trade association in question, but a breach is not in itself an offence.

Hire-Purchase

Advertising of hire-purchase facilities is still regulated by the Advertisements (Hire Purchase) Act, 1967, though shortly to be replaced by Consumer Credit Act provisions. The rules apply to advertisements stating that goods are obtainable by hire-purchase or credit sale and that a deposit is or is not payable, or giving the amount of one or more instalment payments or of a sum stated to be the hire-purchase or total purchase price—but not, in other words, to advertisements which merely say that credit is available. They require that the amount of any necessary deposit be stated directly or as a fraction of a specified sum, and information given as to the amount of each instalment and the total number and frequency of instalments, any instalments payable before delivery, and the cash price and hire-purchase or total purchase price. Breach of these requirements is a criminal offence, but does not affect the validity of any agreement subsequently made. The Consumer Credit Act itself prohibits false and misleading advertisements and it also requires a statement of the true rate of interest, calculated in accordance with formulae provided under the Act. It is an offence under the Act to advertise credit for products or services which are not at the same time available for cash; section 45.

Discrimination

The Race Relations Act, 1976, and Sex Discrimination Act, 1975, forbid advertisements which discriminate on grounds of colour, race, nationality, ethnic or national origin, or sex (as distinct from marital status). Similar legislation in Northern Ireland forbids discrimination on political or religious grounds. Publication of such advertisements is not a criminal offence but may be prevented by injunction, breach of which is punishable.

High Pressure Sales Techniques

We turn now to various methods of selling, apart from advertising as such, which have been found to put undue pressure upon consumers and so are forbidden or restricted by law. The main problem areas are as follows:

The Unsolicited Goods and Services Act
This Act, passed in 1971 and amended in 1975, endorses the common law conclusion that a person who is sent goods or rendered services he has not expressly or impliedly asked for and does not want is not obliged to pay for them; *Felthouse* v. *Bindley*, 1863. But it also meets the need for a more precise statement of the consumer's rights and more stringent control of "inertia sales." It says that when goods are sent to a person without his agreement, and not for use in a trade or business, they become that person's own property—subject to the following rules. His rights of ownership arise only after he has had the goods for six months, and on condition that he has not unreasonably refused to let the sender recover them. Alternatively he can simply give the sender 30 days' notice to recover them, and if they are not recovered within that time they thereupon become his. He is not obliged to take care of the goods in the meantime. Demanding payment for unsolicited goods is a criminal offence, and even sending an invoice is punishable unless the invoice states that no claim for payment is made. The Act also protects people from liability for unwanted directory entries and forbids the sending of indecent publications to individuals who have not asked for them.

The Fair Trading Act and Pyramid Sales
The Act is important here for several reasons. As we shall see it enables the Office of Fair Trading to control the activities of individual traders with a record of "sharp practice." Secondly, various orders have been made under the Act against unfair practices. These forbid the use of certain exclusion clauses in contracts of sale and hire-purchase (Chapter Five), require per-

sons advertising mail order transactions to give their names and addresses, and businessmen selling through newspaper classified advertisement columns to make it clear that the sale is in the course of business. Another Order is proposed to ensure that the buyer knows whether the price includes V.A.T. Thirdly, the Act made special provision for the control of pyramid sales. These are trading schemes under which payments may be made to promoters, either in return for goods which the new recruits are to sell privately at a profit, or in return for promises of larger payments if other participants can be introduced. If the schemes fail considerable hardship might be caused. Sections 118–123 of the Act define such schemes and prohibit participants from making payments so as to qualify for rewards for involving others in the schemes. Pyramid selling regulations made in 1973 define what is to be included in documents inducing people to join, and require that written contracts be given to participants stating their right to withdraw at any time, and on withdrawal within 7 days of joining to recover all payments made. The contract must also record the participant's right to sell back to the promoter any goods purchased from him under the scheme. New participants cannot be required to pay more than £25 for goods, nor can any participant who has not ordered the goods in writing. "Non-returnable" payments taken as security are forbidden, as are charges for training facilities or other promotional services. Breach of the regulations gives rise only to civil liability.

The Consumer Credit Act and "Cooling-off" Provisions

The only parts of this long and complex Act—dealt with at length in "Consumer Credit" in this series—which we are concerned with here are those controlling "doorstep" salesmen and certain other forms of domestic pressure. A credit agreement signed by the consumer in his own home (or anywhere other than at the creditor's or dealer's business premises) following oral negotiations at the shop or at home is called a "cancellable agreement". The rules on such agreements are in sections 64 and 67–74 of the Act. They apply, with exceptions noted below, to all agreements made in this way which extend credit of up to £5,000 to individuals. They give the consumer an opportunity for second thoughts—a "cooling off" period—and the right then to cancel what would otherwise be a binding agreement. His attention must be drawn to his rights in prominently displayed sections of copies of the agreement or by a notice to that effect. He is entitled to one copy on signing the agreement and to another within the following seven days. But if the agreement is already signed by the creditor or owner before the consumer signs it, the latter must be sent a notice of his right to cancel within seven days. If he decides to cancel the agreement he must do so in writing within five days after the day he receives the second copy or notice. Cancellation entitles the consumer to recover any money paid and ends all future obligations, except of course that the creditor or owner is entitled to recover goods delivered, and the consumer must pay for work done or goods supplied "to meet an emergency," or for perishables, or where goods have been supplied which the consumer has already worked into his own land or other property not within the agreement. He may also have to pay up to £1 as fee or commission. If the agreement is for a credit card the card must be returned before his payment can be recovered. In all other cases the consumer can keep any goods delivered until repayment, taking reasonable care of them for up to 21 days after cancellation. When an agreement which involves the consumer giving his own goods in part exchange is cancelled the goods must be returned to him within 10 days of cancellation in essentially the same condition.

The main exception to this otherwise comprehensive protection against doorstep salesmanship is in what the Act calls "small agreements." These are credit sale agreements for less than £30; section 17. An agreement for more than £30 must not be split into two or more agreements below that figure. Other agreements not subject to the cooling-off rules are those for fixed sums which must be repaid in not more than four instalments or for credit which is not extended under a pre-existing arrangement between creditor and dealer and which is to be repaid at not more than one per cent. above the Bank of England Minimum Lending Rate, or 13 per cent., whichever is higher.

Certain other possible domestic pressures are forbidden by sections 49–51. Under section 49 it is illegal to canvass a person away from trade premises to borrow money. Canvassing a consumer to see if he would like overdraft facilities on a current account is, however, permissible. Section 50 forbids canvassing persons under 18 to borrow money or obtain credit. By section 51 credit tokens, except for "small agreements," may only be sent on the consumer's written and signed request unless by way of renewal.

Trading Stamps; Share Pushing; Auction Rigging; Representations as to Disablement; Prospectuses; Banks
Under the Trading Stamps Act, 1964, the same standards of fitness are applied to goods given in return for stamps as in ordinary contracts of sale. Only companies and industrial and provident societies are permitted to operate stamp schemes. Stamps must bear the name of the promoter and a cash value. They are redeemable for cash when they have a face value of more than 25 pence. It is an offence under the Prevention of Fraud (Investments) Act, 1958, as amended by the Protection of Depositors Act, 1963, to sell shares at a person's home without a licence from the Department of Industry unless the seller is a member of a recognised stock exchange or other exempted body. Auction rigging is forbidden by the Mock Auctions Act, 1961, and Auction (Bidding Agreements) Acts, 1927 and 1969. It is illegal for anyone other than a local authority or other authorised institution to canvass for sales by representing that disabled persons will benefit thereby; Trading Representations (Disabled Persons) Acts, 1958 and 1972. Misleading prospectuses are banned by the Companies Act, 1948, and banks can only advertise deposit facilities in accordance with the Banking Act, 1979.

The Office of Fair Trading

We have seen that the aggrieved consumer can sue for damages for breach of contract or negligence, or report various illegal forms of advertising or high pressure techniques to the local Trading Standards Department and hope to receive compensation in the course of any ensuing prosecution. We come now to the third line of approach, that of complaint to the Director-General of the Office of Fair Trading, whose address is Chancery Lane, London. The OFT was established by the Fair Trading Act, 1973. Up to a point the Director might be regarded as Britain's "Consumer Ombudsman," except that he is not empowered to take up the cudgels on behalf of individual consumers. He has nonetheless a vital part to play in consumer protection, and complaints may usefully be made to him even though the results may be indirect and long term.

The Director has the authority to receive information on the working of consumer protection law from all the enforcement agencies concerned and thus has an overview of the number and nature of our complaints. Secondly, he can submit proposals for law reform to an independent body known as the Consumer Protection Advisory Committee which may recommend legislation to the Secretary of State for Trade. We listed above the orders made so far. Breach of an order is a criminal offence, and prosecution is undertaken by the Trading Standards Departments. Thirdly, under sections 34–43 of the Act the Director can exercise a novel form of long term control over the activities of individual traders. If in his view—based on public complaints and information supplied by Trading Standards Departments and the like—a trader has persistently behaved in a way detrimental to the interests of consumers, which involves breach of criminal or civil duties, the Director can seek a written assurance from the trader that he will abandon such conduct. Should the trader refuse to give an assurance, or, having given one, break it, the Director can ask the Restrictive Practices Court or county court to make an order against him. Breach of an order or undertaking given to the court is contempt of court, which could lead to an unlimited fine or prison. If the business in question is one supplying credit facilities, the Director may achieve the same end by refusing to grant the necessary licence.

Another important duty is that of encouraging trade associations to prepare codes of practice for their members to safeguard the interests of consumers; section 124. A dozen or so codes have been agreed between the OFT and a wide range of organisations. They include the Association of Manufacturers of Domestic Electrical Appliances, the Association of British Travel Agents, the Electricity Council, the Vehicle Builders' and Repairers' Association, the Society of Motor Manufacturers' and the Motor Agents' Association, the Association of British Launderers and Drycleaners, the National Association of Shoe Repair Factories, the Footwear Distributors' Federation, the Mail Order Publishers' Authority, and the Radio, Electrical and Television Retailers' Association. Under the latter code, for example, Association members must give a comprehensive 12 month guarantee covering the cost of both parts and labour, supplementing any manufacturers' guarantees. Members unable to repair any appliance under guarantee within 15 days are required to supply a similar appliance to the customer, or where this is impractical, to extend the period of the guarantee by the number of days the customer is deprived of the use of his appliance. Other significant provisions require that where a member is requested to call on a customer to repair an appliance, a first visit should be made within three working days of receiving the request and repairs should be completed within 15 days of the first visit; repairs are to be guaranteed for a minimum period of three months; members will refund deposits for goods that are not available on time and will give receipts, detailed invoices and as much information as possible to customers. Lastly, if there is a dispute between a customer and a member, either can refer the matter to the Secretary of the Association, and, if the problem still cannot be resolved, to the Association's Customer Conciliation Panel which has an independent chairman.

Lastly the Director General is authorised by section 124 to arrange for the publication of general information and advice to consumers. His Office has produced free publicity material explaining its work, publicising the codes, setting out shoppers' rights and duties in various different types of transaction, *e.g.* "Get Smart—Your Complete Guide to Shopping Without Tears," and explaining the Consumer Credit Act. The Office's literature goes to local consumer advice centres, libraries and the like.

Overall therefore the Director's position is clearly a powerful and important one—but his work depends on public support. Although as we said individual consumers are not likely to benefit directly by complaining to him, he can only take action necessary to protect consumers generally if he is kept fully informed of tricks of the trade as and when they are played.

The Advertising Standards Authority

Complaints about advertising, including aspects which are difficult for the law to deal with—questions of taste, morality, intrusion into privacy, and the like—can also be made to the

ASA. This is a voluntary body set up by the advertising industry. It has a board of 12 members, eight of whom are independent of the industry and include consumers' representatives. The Authority's address is 15 Ridgmount Street, London, W.C.1, and it invites complaints by members of the public against advertisements which infringe its Code of Advertising Practice. This is a lengthy document, beginning with the proposition that "all advertisements should be legal, decent, honest and truthful." Summaries are obtainable free from the Authority. Some 3,000–4,000 complaints are received annually. Reports of cases investigated and decided upon are published every two months. If the Code is infringed the sanctions include that very limited amount of adverse publicity and the possible withholding of advertising space or time and loss of trading facilities. The number of infringements may suggest that further legal intervention is necessary, as was envisaged by the Department of Prices and Consumer Protection.

CHAPTER SEVEN

LEGAL AID AND ADVICE : COUNTY COURT PROCEEDINGS

Advisory Services

This little book has been devised to give both consumers and dealers a general idea of the way the law approaches their problems. It would be surprising, however, if it could provide precise answers to individual queries, each in some way different from the next. Faced with a particular problem—of faulty or dangerous goods, shoddy service or misleading advertising—where should the consumer go for more specific guidance? Probably the last thing he wants to do about his problem is go to law, and probably therefore the last person he would think of consulting is a solicitor. This may or may not be a sensible attitude, but it is certainly a very common and understandable one. We should note, therefore, the various agencies which might be able to help him free of charge before we see what court proceedings might involve.

Probably the best known and most used of our consumer advisory agencies—interpreting the word "consumer" in its widest sense—are the Citizens' Advice Bureaux. There are some 700 bureaux all over the country. A perhaps more highly specialised service is provided by the more recently established Consumer Advice Centres, of which there are more than 100, run by local authorities, C.A.Bx. or local consumer groups. Both agencies have been invaluable in giving information, providing mediation services and in many cases securing compensation. Within the past few years about 30 Law Centres have also appeared, offering professional legal services paid for by public funds. If the consumer's problem concerns a nationalised industry he should approach the appropriate consumer council, such as the Electricity Council or Post Officer Users' Council. These are essentially consultative organisations, but may serve a useful purpose in intervening between traders and consumers to secure more satisfactory service.

If conciliation fails, however, or if the consumer prefers either to "go it alone" or to consult the nearest solicitor for more immediate results, what sort of court proceedings may eventually be involved, and what range of costs may he face?

County Courts
Most consumer complaints are dealt with in the county court, which can try claims for up to £2,000—or more by agreement between the parties. Larger claims go to the Queen's Bench Division of the High Court. County courts will be found in all large centres of population and they also sit periodically in many smaller towns. Cases are tried by a judge sitting without a jury, or, if less than £200 is involved, by the court registrar. The registrar is a solicitor, from whom an appeal may be made to the judge. Appeals from the county court are to the Court of Appeal in London on questions of law, but only with leave if the subject matter is worth less than £20, and possibly on questions of fact if the claim involves more than £200. The Scottish equivalent of the county court is the sheriff court, but it does not have the small claims procedures described below.

County courts can only hear cases which are in some way connected with the area they serve. The plaintiff must therefore make his claim either in the court for the district where the defendant lives or carries on business, or where his cause of action arose. Thus if a consumer has a complaint against a finance house because of faulty goods obtained on hire purchase from a local dealer he could sue in that local court.

Claims are begun simply by the plaintiff obtaining a form called a "request" from the county court office and filling it in with particulars of the parties and the nature and amount of his claim. He files this document and his particulars of claim—again drafted in his own words—with the court, paying a small fee for so doing and another for the office's service in issuing the summons to the other side. These court costs should not exceed about £10–£15, depending on the amount claimed. The county court office should be able to help the plaintiff in filling in or drafting the forms, but he might in any case find the Lord Chancellor's Office publication "Small Claims in the County Court" useful, and it is available free from court offices. Another helpful and interesting booklet is "How to sue in the county court," published by the Consumers' Association (whose Personal Service subscribers are, incidentally, entitled to legal advice from that organisation).

Costs

The biggest problem is of course that of the costs likely to arise if the claim is contested. Legal costs are still high. Solicitors' charges are at least £15–£20 an hour, and if barristers are used (as they must be in the High Court, unless the claimant represents himself, but need not be in the county court) the costs will increase considerably. The basic rule is that the loser pays both his own and most of the winner's costs, so that—subject to the small claims provisions we are coming to—there is clearly a point at which it is unwise to pursue a grievance because of the danger of throwing good money after bad.

Over the past few years, however, various new rules have been introduced to simplify county court documentation and procedures and to keep costs within manageable and predictable proportions in small claims. Provision is now made for a pre-trial review by the registrar, whose job it is then to give such directions as seem necessary for securing the just, speedy and economical disposal of the action. In practice he should try to reduce the issues in dispute by finding what common ground there is and what admissions may be made. If a defendant accepts liability at this stage the case is concluded. If he does not appear judgment may be given against him. Reports differ as to the extent to which and spirit in which registrars undertake such reviews. Under the Administration of Justice Act, 1973, either side can ask the court to refer claims for up to £200, or more if the parties agree, to arbitration—with corresponding advantages of speed, informality and privacy. Rules of evidence should not be quite so strictly applied, and the parties should feel more at ease and able to explain their own problems in their own way (though again reports differ as to the way registrars have conducted such proceedings). There is no appeal from an arbitration decision unless the arbitrator mis-states the law or otherwise misconducts himself. The use of legal representation is deliberately discouraged by another new provision which, contrary to the general rule, requires each side to pay its own costs if not more than £200 is claimed or awarded. Exceptions include personal injury claims. If therefore a consumer fights his own battle without a lawyer but loses he will not have to pay more than the small court fees just mentioned. Representation by non-lawyers, *e.g.* local authority consumer protection officials, is permitted. The effect of these reforms should undoubtedly be to make county courts a good deal cheaper and more accessible than they have been.

We should note in passing also the existence of two "independent" small claims courts in London and Manchester. Sponsored originally as research projects in the early 1970s, they have now been taken over by the local authorities. They offer arbitration facilities at very low cost, subject to the agreement of the parties and without the right of legal representation or appeal, and they have been extensively used. Their further development in England and Wales was probably made unnecessary by the changes in county court rules we have just described, but since corresponding changes have not taken place in the jurisdiction of the sheriff court, the Scottish Consumer Council is advocating the establishment of one in Edinburgh or Glasgow, to be available to parties throughout the country. Finally in this connection we should mention again the Powers of Criminal Courts Act, 1973, which enables criminal courts to make compensation orders for the victims of crime and so makes it unnecessary for them to launch separate civil proceedings against the wrongdoer. As we have said this power is particularly beneficial to consumers deceived by misleading advertising.

Legal action, apart from the small claims procedure, however, remains intimidating and expensive, and as indicated above would be prohibitively so for most of us unless outside assistance were available. The Legal Aid and Advice Act of 1949 introduced what was intended as a comprehensive scheme of assistance funded by the State and administered by Area and Local Aid Committees consisting of barristers and solicitors, answerable to the Lord Chancellor. The present law is in the Legal Aid Acts, 1974–79, and regulations thereunder. Different provision is made according to whether the citizen seeks only advice as to his legal rights, or assistance in court action. It will be borne in mind that we are concerned here only with the exercise of civil rights, not the operation of the criminal law.

So far as the advisory aspect is concerned help is given under the "£25 scheme" or "green form scheme." The names of solicitors willing to take part in this scheme are available at local advice centres and general post offices, and signs outside their offices also publicise their services. A member of the public seeking legal advice must fill in an official green form at the solicitor's office to enable the solicitor to decide whether the applicant is within the scheme's financial limits, below. If so he can have up to £25 worth of advice and non-litigious service such as the writing of letters, negotiation, and possibly the obtaining of counsel's opinion. If the solicitor considers that the work required will cost over £25 he must obtain the approval of the Area committee before providing more than the first £25 worth.

Advice under the green form scheme is free if the applicant's "disposable income" is less than £35 a week. His disposable income is assessed after certain deductions for the maintenance of dependants, tax, rates, rent, travelling expenses to and from work, etc. If according to these allowances his income is over £35 but less than £75 a week he must pay proportionately up to £56. If in the event the solicitor's costs exceed the contribution, he has a charge for the excess on any property or money recovered through his assistance. People receiving supplementary benefit or family income supplement are automatically eligible for legal advice, subject to the "disposable capital" rules. Savings must not exceed £600 for an applicant without dependants. Furniture, clothing and tools of trade are disregarded, as is the value of the applicant's house.

The Legal Aid Act, 1979, extends the green form scheme to legal representation in court, subject to the court's approval and to increased liability to contribute towards costs. Applicants outside the scheme must apply first to the Local Legal Aid Committee, which will decide whether they have reasonable grounds for making or defending a claim. A committee of this kind, entrusted with the expenditure of public money and consisting only of practitioners, might be expected to err on the side of caution and to reject applications which appear to concern small or speculative issues, a restriction which does not of course affect more affluent members of society. An appeal against a refusal can be made to the Area Committee. Subject to this and the following financial considerations legal aid is given to any individual for both trial and appeal proceedings, excluding those involving defamation and the many specialised types of case dealt with by judicial or administrative tribunals, such as industrial or rent or insurance tribunals, other than the Lands Tribunal. Legal aid may be given free of charge if the Supplementary Benefits Commission to which the case is then referred assesses the applicant's disposable income at less than £1,500 a year and his disposable capital at less than £1,200. He may be required to make a contribution to the Legal Aid Fund of up to a quarter of the amount by which his income exceeds £1,500, within a disposable income limit of £3,600 and/or of the amount by which his disposable capital exceeds £1,200, depending on the total amount of costs incurred. If his disposable capital is more than £2,500 he is usually regarded as outside the scheme, unless he seems unlikely to be able to proceed with the case without help. The above figures are those effective in 1979. The limits are increased annually.

There are other problems apart from eligibility. The policies of the Act regarding costs incurred and damages awarded in particular cases can be equally important. So for example an assisted person who loses his case may be ordered to pay the costs of the other side, so far as is reasonable in the light of his means and the conduct of the case. Since by definition the assisted party's means are limited the successful but unassisted person could be very much out of pocket—or would be so but for sections 13 and 14 of the Act which permit payment of costs out of the Legal Aid Fund if otherwise "severe financial hardship" would result. This rule should not be so strictly applied as to exclude people of modest means who would find it hard to bear their own costs; *Hanning* v. *Maitland*, 1970. Conversely even if the assisted person wins his claim his legal difficulties are not necessarily resolved thereby. The rule in section 9 is that if any costs paid by the other side do not cover the costs incurred by the Legal Aid Fund in fighting the case, the Fund has a first charge for the deficit on any property or money recovered in the action. The effect of this rule may be to deprive the plaintiff of most or all of even a quite substantial award, so nullifying the whole proceedings and indeed the ultimate purpose of the legislation. Some measure of reform is undoubtedly necessary in this respect. On the other hand again if a consumer conducts a case himself—as he is able to do—he can recover costs representing work done and losses incurred; Litigants in Person (Costs and Expenses) Act, 1975.

The Legal Aid Act obviously has its limitations. In particular its financial limits, though periodically revised, have led to the suggestion that the old saying "There's one law for the rich and another for the poor" should be changed, and should now be "There's one law for the rich and the poor, and another for the middle class." Certainly people whose incomes put them just beyond the reach of the scheme, with gross annual earnings of say £5,000–£6,000 upwards, must be most reluctant to go to law simply because of the costs involved—unless of course they can use the small claims procedure. It is equally true that those who are eligible may not be benefited either because they do not know about their legal rights in the first place, or about the help which is in fact available. But perhaps this little book and others like it can play some small part in helping to resolve these problems.

INDEX